SHUT UP THE LIES IN YOUR HEAD

A WOMAN'S GUIDE TO OVERCOMING TOXIC THOUGHTS AND ANXIETY WITH LIFE-TRANSFORMING TRUTHS

1ST EDITION 2024

MATAILA HAIRSTON

MATAILA

CONTENTS

INTRODUCTION

Do you ever feel like you're battling an invisible enemy that whispers doubts, fears, negativity, and untruths into your mind? Recent studies reveal that an overwhelming number of women grapple with toxic thoughts daily, significantly impacting their mental wellness and spiritual health. It's estimated that an astonishing 85% of our thoughts can be negative or self-defeating. It's no wonder our generation is witnessing a rapid rise in mental health cases globally! This can be attributed to several factors, including increased social and economic pressures, the pervasive influence of social media, and the aftermath of the global COVID-19 pandemic. These elements have collectively heightened levels of anxiety, stress, and isolation. Additionally, the fast-paced, high-demand nature of modern life often leaves us with insufficient time for rest and self-care, exacerbating mental health issues. So those whispers of doubt about your abilities, fear about your future, and untruths about your circumstances are not an isolated silent battle—it's an epidemic!

Our battlefield is in our minds, where beliefs are formed, challenged, and solidified.

As Christians, it is crucial to remember that while we live in this world, we are not to conform to its values and systems but are to be transformed by God's truth and Holy Spirit. Daily, we face a real enemy determined to undermine our identity in Christ, to prevent us from effectively participating in God's kingdom plans for our lives. Even in this information age, his strategy mirrors his tactics from Genesis 3, to sow seeds of lies that cause doubt about God's promises and plans for us. He understands that the mind is the center of thought, reason, and decision-making, encompassing the formation and holding of our beliefs. If he can convince us to believe his lies, he can keep us subdued and preoccupied with worldly distractions, preventing us from fulfilling the Kingdom of God's purposes for which we were created. Our battlefield is in our minds, where beliefs are formed, challenged, and solidified. Victory or defeat hinges on what we believe, which in turn determines our mental wellness or lack thereof.

Mental wellness refers to a state of well-being wherein an individual realizes their abilities, can cope with the everyday stresses of life, can work productively, and can make a meaningful contribution to their community. It encompasses a positive state of mental health, where an individual experiences a sense of balance, resilience, and the ability to thrive in various aspects of life.

The critical aspects of mental wellness include:

1. Emotional Well-being: The ability to understand and manage emotions, maintain a positive outlook, and recover from setbacks;

2. Psychological Well-being: Engaging in activities that promote mental stimulation, creativity, and intellectual growth;
3. Social Well-being: Building and maintaining healthy relationships, having a sense of belonging, and contributing to the community;
4. Resilience: The capacity to cope with stress, adversity, and challenges in a healthy and constructive manner;
5. Self-acceptance: Recognizing and appreciating your worth, abilities, and limitations.

Achieving mental wellness involves adopting healthy lifestyle habits, such as regular physical activity, balanced nutrition, adequate sleep, stress management techniques, and seeking support when needed. It also includes engaging in activities that promote joy, relaxation, and fulfillment.

The decision to write this book began as I faced and overcame my own mental wellness challenges, which had me navigating through battlefields of relentless whispers of inadequacy, uncertainty, and falsehoods, a struggle you might find all too familiar. My first response was to ignore these negative thoughts, which provided no relief since those ideas were shelved for retrieval later. Shifting my focus to something else as a distraction offered only temporary respite, failing to address the root cause of the underlying feelings of uncertainty, fear, and concerns. These unaddressed thoughts would then spiral, exacerbating the anxiety and manifesting as stress. Spiraling thoughts start as a minor concern but then escalate rapidly, leading to a cycle of worry. During this dark season, my anxiety escalated to a point where I sought relief through medication.

Anxiety medications, such as selective serotonin reuptake inhibitors (SSRIs) and benzodiazepines, work by balancing neurotransmitters in the brain, which can reduce anxiety and improve mood. However, it's important to note that these medications address the chemical aspects of anxiety and not the underlying causes of anxiety. So, they are typically most beneficial when combined with other treatments, such as therapy, lifestyle changes, and stress management techniques. So, while these medications provided me with a temporary but much-needed reprieve from the overwhelming pressure and circumstances, they fell short of offering the mental transformation I needed to confront and dismantle the relentless whispers of lies that brought about the anxiety.

During a period of deep prayer and seeking wisdom from spiritual mentors, I identified my struggles with stress, anxiety, and burnout as signs of misalignment with God's truth and plan in certain areas of my life. The breakthrough came when I recognized that the only way to silence the lies in my mind and conquer the toxic thoughts was by wielding a weapon far more potent than any lie—the infallible word of God. Hebrews 4:12 reveals the power of God's word, stating it is "alive and active, sharper than any double-edged sword, it penetrates even to dividing soul and spirit, joints and marrow; it judges the thoughts and attitudes of the heart." By examining my thoughts and deliberately challenging each falsehood with scriptural truth, I started reclaiming my peace, experiencing a shift that affected my mental wellness and whole being.

"SHUT UP The Lies in Your Head: A Woman's Guide to Conquering Toxic Thoughts and Anxiety with Life Transforming Truths" is more than just a book; it's a lifeline thrown into the chaotic seas of your mind. It shows you that the battlefield of our thoughts is not only real but also winnable. The truths of the Holy Scriptures have the power to dismantle lies, and when combined with scientific insights into mental wellness, they form a powerful duo that can set you on a path to freedom. Medication-free freedom.

In case you were wondering why I refer to mental wellness as opposed to mental health, the term "mental health" is often used in clinical settings to address the diagnosis, treatment, and management of mental disorders and illnesses. In contrast, "mental wellness" is often used in holistic and preventive contexts to emphasize proactive, positive approaches to maintaining mental well-being and preventing mental health issues. Both terms are important and relevant, and together, they represent a comprehensive approach to understanding and promoting mental well-being.

Our enemy is determined to infiltrate our minds, to make us feel helpless, overwhelmed, and incapable of making a difference for the kingdom of God.

I pray that through this book, which merges scriptural wisdom with proven mental wellness strategies to create a roadmap for overcoming toxic thoughts, countless women will realize that our generation's greatest spiritual battle is being fought between our ears. God has given us a choice: either life or death, and the thoughts we allow to occupy our mental space regularly ultimately become the choices we make—thoughts leading to a life of peace or thoughts leading to turmoil and spiritual death. Our enemy is determined to infiltrate our minds, to make us feel helpless, overwhelmed, and incapable of making a difference for the kingdom of God. However, when we submit our minds to Christ, the promises and goodness of God flood our lives in remarkable ways.

Structured to be relatable and immensely practical, this book will help you recognize the common lies that plague our minds, such as feelings of unworthiness, fears about the future, and doubts about one's abilities. Each chapter is designed to confront these false-hoods with the truth of God's Word, supported by scientific research. I have seen the dark cloud that doubt can cause, yet I have emerged into the light of truth. May this book inspire you to do the same.

Whether you are a young adult just starting your journey of faith or a seasoned believer who has faced numerous battles, this book speaks to you. It is crafted for all women who yearn to break free from mental shackles and step into a life marked by peace and confidence in who they are in Christ.

As we embark on this journey together through the pages of this book, approach each chapter with an open heart, ready to challenge the lies and embrace the transformative power of truth. Our battle is not just about fighting negative thoughts; it's about winning the war and claiming the joyous, fulfilled life you are meant to live as a powerful instrument in the Kingdom of God. Join me, and let's begin this journey to shut the lies up and amplify the truth that sets us free.

CHAPTER 1: IDENTIFYING AND UNDERSTANDING TOXIC THOUGHTS

"A toxic thought is any idea that undermines your sense of self-worth, distorts your perception of reality, or keeps you from forming healthy relationships with others and God."

From the moment you wake up, a dialogue begins in your head. Who is that voice you are conversing with? Have you ever considered that your thoughts might just have their own life? Like those little cartoon characters with pitchforks and halos, whispering into each ear, vying for your attention. It sounds amusing, but the reality? Not so much. Those whispers can often feel more like shouts, especially the negative ones that seem eager to point out every flaw or mistake. In this chapter, we will tackle these intrusive guests, understand their roots, and learn how to show them the door politely (or not so politely).

Our mind is a battlefield, and every thought we entertain is a soldier in the fight for our mental wellness and spiritual health.

But before we can command these soldiers, we need to know them well. Let's start by dissecting these toxic thoughts—the sneaky culprits behind much of our mental unrest.

1.1 THE ANATOMY OF A TOXIC THOUGHT: UNDERSTANDING ITS ROOTS AND IMPACTS

Defining Toxic Thoughts

So, what exactly makes a thought toxic? Think of a toxic thought as any idea that undermines your sense of self-worth, distorts your perception of reality, or keeps you from forming healthy relationships with others and God. These are the thoughts that whisper, "You're not good enough," "You can't do this," or "You don't matter." They're like weeds in the garden of your mind, growing wild and threatening to choke out all the good thoughts.

Toxic thoughts often lead to a cascade of negativity that affects how you view yourself and interact with the world. They can sabotage your work efforts, disrupt relationships, and make you feel distant from your spiritual community. Recognizing these thoughts is the first step toward pulling them up by the roots before they do more damage.

If not addressed, toxic thoughts can become spiraling thoughts. Spiraling thoughts are a pattern of repetitive and often negative thinking that can intensify anxiety and stress. Like mentioned earlier, these thoughts typically start with a minor concern and escalate rapidly, leading to a cycle of worry and fear. For example, a person might begin by worrying about a small mistake at work, which then spirals into fears about job security, financial stability, and future prospects. This pattern can be challenging to break and may require strategies such as meditation, cognitive-behavioral techniques, and sometimes professional support to manage if you struggle to handle them independently.

Biological Basis of Toxic Thoughts

Let's delve into the science behind these thoughts for a moment and explore the intricate workings of your remarkable brain. When you think a thought, your brain fires neurons in patterns and sequences. If a particular idea is repeated—like those pesky toxic ones—your brain begins to use this pathway more, making it easier for that thought to be triggered. It's like a trail in the woods that becomes a well-worn path after many people walk on it.

This neural activity can physically impact your brain's structure—yes, your thoughts can reshape your brain! Prolonged negativity can lead to heightened activity in the amygdala (the brain's fear center) and decrease connectivity in areas responsible for mood regulation and cognitive function. This biological change is why breaking the cycle of toxic thinking can feel as challenging as breaking any physical habit—it's literally hardwired into your brain's structure.

Emotional Consequences of Toxic Thoughts

Living with toxic thoughts is like walking around with a personal rain cloud. Emotionally, these thoughts can stir up a whole storm of negative feelings: anxiety, fear, sadness, and even depression. Each toxic thought reinforces this emotional weather pattern, making it harder to see the sunshine, even on bright days. These emotions are not just fleeting feelings; they affect your everyday functioning. Anxiety can make it hard to make decisions or start new projects. Fear might stop you from taking healthy risks. Sadness can pull you away from social activities. Before you know it, these emotions can start dictating your life choices, keeping you from pursuing your goals and dreams.

Spiritual Ramifications of Toxic Thoughts

On a spiritual level, toxic thoughts can be particularly damaging. They can make you feel unworthy of God's love or disconnected from His presence. Thoughts like "I'm not a good enough Christian" or "God couldn't possibly forgive me" can create a barrier between you and the deep, fulfilling relationship with God that you desire and deserve.

These thoughts challenge your spiritual identity, which is grounded in who God says you are, not in your mistakes or shortcomings. They disrupt your spiritual growth and can keep you from participating fully in your faith community, serving others, and experiencing the joy of living a life aligned with God's purposes.

Understanding the anatomy of toxic thoughts is crucial because it empowers you to start making changes. Knowledge is power; with this knowledge, you're better equipped to transform your mind, heal your heart, and deepen your spiritual connection. The mind is like a garden where better thoughts can flourish, but only if we're willing to do the gardening. So, let's roll up our sleeves and get to work.

Social Effects of Toxic Thoughts

Toxic thoughts, such as persistent negativity, self-doubt, and feelings of unworthiness, can significantly impact an individual's social interactions and relationships. These thoughts can lead to social withdrawal and isolation, as individuals may feel inadequate or fear judgment and rejection from others. Over time, this isolation can erode social support networks, leaving individuals without the crucial emotional support needed to cope with life's challenges. This lack of social interaction can further reinforce toxic thoughts, creating a vicious cycle that exacerbates feelings of loneliness and depression.

Moreover, toxic thoughts can strain existing relationships. Individuals who constantly battle negative self-perceptions may struggle to communicate effectively and may misinterpret the intentions and actions of others, leading to misunderstandings and conflicts. They may also project their insecurities onto others, damaging trust and intimacy in close relationships. Additionally, the stress and emotional turmoil caused by toxic thoughts can manifest as irritability or defensiveness, making it difficult for others to offer support or maintain a positive relationship. Overall, the social ramifications of toxic thoughts are profound, as they not only harm the individual's mental health but also disrupt their ability to form and maintain healthy, supportive relationships.

The Mean Girl Syndrome: A Fruit of Toxic Thoughts

Let's bring it home now. We have all either witnessed or experienced mean girls. Some of you beloved readers were, or dare I say, are, mean girls! But have no fear. This is a safe place. We are all on a journey.

The "mean girl syndrome," characterized by aggressive, manipulative, and exclusionary behavior among girls and young women, can often be traced back to underlying toxic thoughts and insecurities. These behaviors are frequently a manifestation of internal struggles with self-worth, jealousy, and fear. Girls who exhibit mean girl tendencies may harbor toxic thoughts such as "I'm not good enough," "I need to be better than others to be valued," or "If I don't control my social environment, I'll be excluded." These harmful beliefs can drive them to act out in ways that undermine others to protect or elevate their status.

Toxic thoughts can lead to a constant need for validation and a fear of vulnerability, pushing these girls and women to engage in mean-spirited behaviors as a defense mechanism. By putting others down, spreading rumors, or creating cliques, mean girls attempt to mask their insecurities and maintain a semblance of control and superiority. This behavior creates a toxic social environment where competition, exclusion, and bullying thrive, further perpetuating the cycle of negative thoughts and behaviors.

Moreover, the mean girl syndrome is reinforced by societal and cultural influences that prioritize external validation and social status over genuine self-esteem and kindness. Media portrayals of popularity, beauty, and success often glorify mean girl behavior, implicitly suggesting that such tactics effectively achieve social power and recognition. As a result, girls internalize these messages, leading to the normalization of toxic behaviors and the reinforcement of their underlying insecurities.

The social ramifications of mean girl syndrome are significant, affecting both the individuals exhibiting these behaviors and those targeted by them. Victims of mean-girl tactics can suffer from decreased self-esteem, anxiety, and depression, leading to long-term psychological impacts. To this day, I still vividly remember how I felt when I was intentionally isolated in high school by a mean girl clique, which left me questioning my worth as a mere teenager. For the mean girls themselves, perpetuating toxic behaviors can result in shallow, untrusting relationships and a continued cycle of negative self-perception and insecurity all through adulthood.

1.2 COMMON TOXIC THOUGHTS AND THEIR ORIGINS

Our minds can often become a maze filled with misleading thoughts. These aren't just your run-of-the-mill negative thoughts;

they're deeper, quietly chipping away at our spiritual health and making us question our worth, devotion, and ability to meet our responsibilities. Bringing these insidious thoughts into the light and understanding their origins is vital.

The Devil - The Father of Lies and Originator of Misleading Thoughts

The Bible identifies the devil as the father of lies and the originator of deceit. In John 8:44, Jesus, responding to his critics who rejected his teachings, says, "You belong to your father, the devil, and you want to carry out your father's desires. He was a murderer from the beginning, not holding to the truth, for there is no truth in him. When he lies, he speaks his native language, for he is a liar and the father of lies." This scripture highlights the devil's fundamental nature as a deceiver, always seeking to undermine our faith and lead us astray.

The misleading thoughts that invade our minds originate from the devil's influence. These thoughts are not merely negative musings; they are strategic attacks designed to weaken our spiritual foundation and prevent us from fulfilling our purposes. By planting seeds of doubt, fear, and inadequacy, the devil makes us question who we are, our worth, and our ability to fulfill our God-given responsibilities.

Below is a list of examples of toxic thoughts countless women deal with and their usual origins.

Toxic Thoughts About Yourself

- "I'm not good enough."

This toxic thought often stems from constant comparison to others, valuing other people's opinions over what God says, unrealistic societal standards of success, and past failures. Believing that you need to attain perfection to deserve love and respect is a toxic lie designed to discourage you, as perfection is an impossible standard to meet.

- "I'm unlovable."

Experiences of past relationship traumas, negative self-perception, and lack of affirmation can lead to the belief that one is unworthy of love. This thought can be deeply rooted in childhood experiences and reinforced by unhealthy adult relationships.

- "I'm a failure."

Unmet personal goals, critical feedback from others, and high self-expectations often lead to this toxic thought. The pressure to succeed in multiple areas of life can make any setback feel like a monumental failure.

- "I can continue to live in sin and not face consequences because God is good."

This thought often originates from a combination of factors, including a misunderstanding of moral and spiritual consequences, popular culture influences that downplay the severity of sin, and personal rationalizations. For example, someone might think, "If no one finds out, it doesn't matter," failing to recognize their actions' internal and spiritual impact. Or, "I deserve this because I've been through a lot," or "Everyone else is doing it, so why shouldn't I?" This self-justification forgets that every choice we make today will have consequences. Consequences now, in the near future, with the next generation, or on judgment day. Either way, there is a price to pay.

Toxic Thoughts About A Significant Other

- "They don't really care about me."

Misunderstandings, miscommunication, unfulfilled emotional desires, and previous relationship encounters often fuel this belief. We tend to feel unseen or undervalued when our needs are not recognized or met.

"I'm better off alone."

Fear of vulnerability, previous heartbreak, and a perceived lack of support can make isolation seem safer than finding a God-ordained partner. Despising small beginnings and being impatient can also lead to the misconception that solitude is preferable.

- "I will only be truly happy once I have a husband."

Societal and cultural norms value marriage as a source of fulfillment for women. Media, traditional gender roles, and family or community pressures reinforce this idea. Personal experiences, such as past relationships and feelings of loneliness, further contribute to the belief that marital status is key to happiness. We forget that marriage's highest and ultimate purpose is to glorify God, not to make us happy.

- "My husband is responsible for my happiness."

Media narratives portray romantic relationships and marriage as the primary source of a woman's happiness. Pop culture frequently depicts spouses as responsible for each other's emotional fulfillment. Personal experiences, such as unmet emotional needs and the desire for companionship, further reinforce this belief.

Toxic Thoughts About Your Body

- "I'm ugly."

Media portrayals of beauty, peer comparison, and body shaming experiences are primary contributors. Society often dictates narrow standards of beauty, leaving many women feeling inadequate.

- "I'm fat/too skinny/my butts too small/too big."

Popular culture's beauty standards, comparing yourself with others, critical comments from others, and self-criticism foster this toxic thought. Women are frequently bombarded with messages that equate worth with appearance.

Toxic Thoughts About Your Parenting

- "I'm a bad mother."

Parenting challenges, comparison to other parents, and past mistakes fuel this thought. The ideal of the "perfect mother" creates unrealistic expectations that are impossible to meet, contributing to feelings of inadequacy.

- "My children are failures."

Comparing your children to other people's children, unmet parental expectations, and academic/social pressures can lead to this belief. Parents sometimes project their insecurities and fears onto their children. Placing unfair, rigid milestone expectations on your children can also spark toxic thoughts.

- "My children don't appreciate me."

Lack of communication, generational misunderstandings, and cultural expectations can create feelings of being unappreciated. The gap between parental efforts and children's recognition can be disheartening.

Toxic Thoughts About Your Career or Lack Thereof

- "I'm stuck in a dead-end job."

Career dissatisfaction, lack of advancement opportunities, and peer comparison often foster this thought. Frustration develops and triggers toxic thoughts when you feel undervalued or trapped in a role that doesn't align with your aspirations or purpose.

- "I'll never be successful."

Past professional setbacks, lack of support, and internalized failure contribute to this toxic thought. The pressure to succeed in a competitive environment and constantly trying to keep up with the Joneses can be overwhelming. Lacking a clear vision for the future and goals frequently leads to feelings of dissatisfaction and unfulfillment.

Toxic Thoughts About Money

- "I'll never be financially secure."

Personal experiences, societal influences, and psychological factors can deeply ingrain this fear. Personal financial struggles, family backgrounds marked by instability, and challenging economic environments can exacerbate feelings of inadequacy. Societal pressures, including media portrayals of wealth and peer comparisons, can also exacerbate feelings of inadequacy.

- "I don't deserve wealth."

This belief is fostered by low self-worth, societal views on wealth, and past financial mistakes. Women may feel unworthy of financial success due to deep-seated cultural narratives.

Toxic Thoughts About Your Health

- "I'll never be healthy."

Chronic health issues, family health history, and adverse health experiences can lead to this thought. Ongoing health challenges can create a sense of hopelessness when one fails to recognize the promises and possibilities of divine healing.

- "I'm too busy to take care of myself."

Overwhelming responsibilities, a lack of self-prioritization, and societal expectations that women juggle multiple roles contribute to this toxic thought. Women often place their well-being last on their list of priorities.

Toxic Thoughts About Your Home Environment

- "My home is always a mess."

Overwhelming household tasks, lack of support, and high cleanliness standards can make maintaining a tidy home feel impossible. The expectation to manage a perfect home can be burdensome.

- "I can't create a happy home."

Past family dynamics, comparison to others, and stress contribute to this belief. Creating a peaceful home environment can seem out of reach when faced with daily challenges.

Toxic Thoughts About Other Areas of Life

- "I'll never find balance in my life."

Overcommitment, lack of time management, and societal pressure to "do it all" contribute to this thought. Balancing work, family, and personal time can be overwhelming.

- "I'm always going to struggle."

Past hardships, ongoing life challenges, and a pessimistic outlook can lead to this belief. Feeling stuck in a cycle of struggle can be deeply discouraging.

Such thoughts can escalate, leading to a spiritual identity crisis.

And as if carrying the burdens of all these lies wasn't enough, then comes the mother of all the lies.

- "A true believer wouldn't experience anxiety or depression."

This idea is particularly harmful as it not only questions our faith but also dismisses our emotional struggles as a lack of spirituality, which is far from the truth. Jesus acknowledged that Christians would face tribulations as they journey through life and pursue the Kingdom of God. In John 16:33, He said, "In this world, you will have trouble. But take heart! I have overcome the world." This statement affirms that hardships, including anxiety and depression, can be a part of the Christian experience and not a sign of weak faith.

Jesus reassured His followers that despite these challenges, they could find peace in Him, for He has conquered the ultimate struggles of the world. His words encourage believers to persevere, knowing Christ understands and validates their trials.

Digging deeper, many of these toxic thoughts are rooted in experiences that stretch back to childhood or early adulthood. It could be a critical comment from a loved one that stuck or a past failure that scarred our self-esteem. Sometimes, it's misconceived teachings that we picked up along the way—ideas about God's character or our role in His plan that aren't quite biblically sound. For instance, being taught that God's love must be earned can lead us to believe that every mistake might remove us from His grace, a notion far from the truth of unconditional divine love.

By understanding the origins of these toxic thoughts, we can begin to untangle the knots in our minds. With each thread pulled, we find a little more freedom, room for grace, and a much-needed reminder that we are all works in progress, loved by God not because we are perfect but because we are His.

1.3 PSYCHOLOGICAL TRIGGERS AND BIBLICAL RESPONSES TO ANXIETY

Recall for a moment those situations that quicken your pulse and send your mind into a frenzy. It may be the anticipation of speaking to an audience, the anxious wait for feedback on a project, or the daunting task of juggling family, career, and countless other duties. Anxiety is more than a modern-day catchphrase; it's a tangible aspect of everyday life, especially when familiar negative thoughts begin their relentless chorus. Identifying the origins of this anxiety and formulating a strategy grounded in faith can alleviate our daily struggles and strengthen our spiritual fortitude.

First things first: identifying triggers. This endeavor requires you to become a detective in your own life. Triggers can be as blatant as a stressful job or as subtle as an offhand comment reminding you of a past hurt. They can come from a place of genuine danger or irrational fears. Understanding these triggers is like mapping the minefield of your mind; once you know where the mines are, you can navigate more safely. For instance, if you realize that scrolling through social media first thing in the morning spikes your anxiety, you can adjust your routine to include a more calming, wholesome start.

Cognitive-Behavioral Techniques With A Christian Twist

Now, let's armor up with cognitive-behavioral techniques with a twist—let's weave in our Christian faith. This method involves identifying anxious thoughts, assessing their accuracy, and then countering them with truth. Here's where it gets beautifully biblical. When a thought like "I'm failing at everything" pops up, challenge it with rational evidence (like remembering your recent successes) and spiritual truth. Remind yourself of scriptures like Philippians 4:13, "I can do all things through Christ who strengthens me." It's about training your mind to capture those rogue thoughts and hold them up against the light of God's truth, seeing if they really hold up.

Turning our attention to Scripture reveals a treasure trove of verses and spiritual disciplines designed to still the tumult of anxiety. Psalm 94:19, for example, "When my anxious thoughts multiply within me, Your consolations delight my soul," serves not merely as an ancient scripture but as a testament to God's steadfast presence and comfort amidst our turmoil. Embedding such scriptures into our daily meditation practice elevates them beyond mere text to become a vital source of strength. Engaging in meditation on these divine truths can range from quietly reflecting on them to more immersive, prayerful contemplation where we invite the Holy Spirit to breathe life into these words, allowing them to minister to our hearts deeply.

Prayer is our direct line to divine peace. It's not just about presenting requests or pouring out our troubles, although both are essential. It's also about realignment and reaffirmation of who we are. Regular prayer and meditation foster a state of mental equilibrium, not because they remove the source of anxiety, but because they shift our focus from the problems to the Problem Solver. They remind us that we are not alone in our struggles—far from it. Our prayers connect us to a power infinitely greater than any anxiety-inducing circumstance.

The Bible reassures us of our identity as God's children and our relationship with our Heavenly Father. Romans 8:15-16 says, "The Spirit you received does not make you slaves so that you live in fear again; rather, the Spirit you received brought about your adoption to sonship. And by Him, we cry, 'Abba, Father.' The Spirit Himself testifies with our spirit that we are God's children." This scripture underscores our intimate relationship with God, emphasizing that through prayer, we can approach Him with the confidence and trust of beloved children. This connection provides profound comfort and strength, enabling us to face our challenges with the assurance of His love and support.

Let's look at a case study to bring this to life. Consider Sarah, a middle school teacher dealing with significant job stress. Her trigger? Classroom evaluations. They made her doubt her abilities and spiked her anxiety. By identifying this trigger, Sarah began meditative prayer right before each evaluation, focusing on scriptures that affirmed her capability and God's presence. Over time, her anxiety decreased, and her performance improved, reflecting her newfound confidence. This change wasn't overnight, nor was it done by her strength alone—it was a daily renewal of mind and spirit that shifted her perspective fundamentally.

As we navigate through our scenarios of anxiety, remember that our approach can be both clinical and spiritual. By identifying our triggers, applying cognitive-behavioral strategies, immersing ourselves in Scripture, and committing to regular prayer, we engage in a holistic battle against anxiety. This isn't just about coping—it's about transforming our minds, one truth-filled thought at a time. Remember, the goal here is not to eliminate anxiety completely—that's a tall order in our unpredictable world —but to equip ourselves so thoroughly with the truth that anxiety loses its power to control our lives and steal our peace and joy.

1.4 THE ROLE OF MEDIA AND CULTURE IN SHAPING OUR SELF-IMAGE

The pervasive influence of media and popular culture in our lives often feels like a well-meaning relative constantly offering unso-licited advice. From the billboards we drive past to the shows we binge-watch on lazy evenings and even in the palm of our hands through social media, its influence is relentless. For women, espe-cially, wading through a flood of unrealistic expectations and distorted self-images that seem to whisper, "This is what you should look like" and "This is how you should live" is exhausting, to say the least. Let's unpack this and find a way to navigate this landscape while keeping our self-esteem and spiritual values intact.

First up, media portrayals. Whether it's movies, TV shows, or Instagram feeds, the representation of women can be... well, let's just say, less than realistic. Airbrushed to perfection, flawlessly styled, and often depicted in roles that scream 'having it all,' these portrayals can skew our perception of what's normal and attainable. For Christian women, this skew can be even more pronounced. Where are the representations of women who are strong in their faith? The ones who find beauty in humility, service, and the joy of the Lord? These qualities are often overshadowed by glitz, glam, and an overwhelming focus on external achievements and appearances.

Then, there's the cultural narrative—good old societal expectations. The myth of the 'perfect Christian woman' looms large. She's that superwoman who juggles multiple responsibilities—career, home, community—without breaking a sweat or smudging her eyeliner. She exudes a calm presence with no visible evidence of challenges or turmoil. It's as if Martha Stewart and Mother Teresa had a love child!

I am not suggesting we need to bleed all over the place when we are hurting just to show balance in the realities of the different shades of our lives. However, we must be cautious not to set a standard so high that it sets women up for inevitable failure and guilt. In reality, no one can seamlessly balance all aspects of life without facing struggles and imperfections. This idealized version of the 'perfect Christian woman' ignores the messiness of real life and the grace of God that meets us in our weaknesses. It's essential to recognize this myth for what it is—a damaging and unrealistic portrayal that can hinder rather than help our spiritual and personal growth.

Living a life in pursuit of appearances of perfection can feed toxic thoughts of inadequacy and failure. This expectation emphasizes performance and outward appearance, missing the truth that faith often involves struggle and imperfection. Ecclesiastes 3:11

reminds us that "He has made everything beautiful in its time," highlighting that God's work in our lives is a process. Our walk of faith may not always be neat or attractive, but God transforms and redeems each moment according to His perfect timing.

So, how do we resist these negative influences? It starts with developing a critical eye. Next time you consume media, take a moment to ask yourself, "Whose standard am I measuring this against?" and "Is this uplifting, or does it make me feel inadequate?" Question the source and the intent behind what you're consuming. Remember, just because something is popular doesn't mean it aligns with your values or God's best for you.

Promoting positive media consumption is not about avoidance; it's about choice. Choose to fill your feeds and screen time with content that enriches your life and affirms your values. Follow platforms and influencers who promote positive self-image, accurate-to-life representations, and inspirational content. Books, podcasts, and even certain TV shows can offer refreshing narratives that empower rather than diminish. For instance, consider subscribing to Christian blogs focusing on women's issues or streaming services offering faith-based programming. Instead of delving into the real lives of the women of today's reality shows, fill your digital library with books that delve into the real lives of women in the Bible, offering insights into how to navigate life's challenges with faith and grace.

Navigating media and cultural expectations isn't about shielding yourself from the world; it's about equipping yourself to interact with it in a way that strengthens rather than diminishes your faith and self-image and allows you to shine Christ's light in you, not dim it. By consciously choosing where and how to engage, you assert control over your mental environment, just like you do with your physical environment. You wouldn't keep a vase you hated just because it was a gift, right? Okay, let's try again. You wouldn't put a vase you hated as the centerpiece above your living room mantle just because it was a gift, would you? Similarly, you don't have to keep a subscription or follow a feed that feeds you lies about who you should be.

In this age of information overload, being selective is not just advisable; it's essential! It's about clinging to what is good, true, honorable, and uplifting—filtering out the noise and lies and tuning into the truth. Filtering what you allow yourself to be exposed to isn't just about mental wellness but spiritual steward-ship. The battlefield is between our ears, ladies! It's about making sure that what enters your mind can pass through the filter of Philippians 4:8, which urges us to think about whatever is true, noble, right, pure, lovely, admirable, excellent, or praiseworthy. Let these be the benchmarks for your media consumption, and watch as your self-image transforms from being popular culture-defined to Kingdom culture-defined.

1.5 IDENTIFYING PERSONAL TRIGGERS THROUGH SELF-REFLECTION AND PRAYER

Discovering the sources of our inner unrest can be surprisingly straightforward. Those triggers, the subtle sparks that ignite a storm of toxic thoughts, are often hidden in plain sight within our daily lives. Uncovering these hidden catalysts may seem challeng-ing, but rest assured, through thoughtful self-reflection, dedicated journaling, and earnest prayer, we can find and effectively navigate these triggers with divine grace and wisdom.

Let's start by talking about self-reflection, a tool as valuable as any treasure map. Self-reflection involves taking a step back from the canvas of our lives to see the broader picture. It's about asking ourselves introspective questions like, "When do I most often feel inadequate?" or "What situations leave me drained or doubting my faith?" It's not about navel-gazing or stewing in our thoughts but rather about observing our mental and emotional patterns with the curiosity of a child and the kindness of a friend.

Consider the practice of daily reflection—a simple yet profound technique. Each evening, take a few minutes to think back over your day. Which events or interactions triggered negative feelings or toxic thoughts? Was it a comment from a colleague or spouse, a stressful situation at home, or perhaps something more subtle, like neglecting your morning routine? Identifying these triggers is like being a detective in your own life, and the clues you uncover are invaluable for the next steps of journaling and prayer.

Now, let's talk about journaling. If self-reflection is the detective work, journaling is the detailed report you compile. It's a space to document and reflect on your findings without judgment. Start by keeping a daily thought journal. Whenever you notice a toxic thought creeping in, write it down along with what triggered it. Over time, you'll begin to see patterns. You'll notice that certain situations, people, or even times of day consistently lead to negative thinking. So, an intentional journal isn't just busywork; it's creating a roadmap for your mental and spiritual journey. By tracking your thoughts and triggers, you're laying down a trail of breadcrumbs to find your way back to peace and clarity.

Integrating prayer into this process is like having a direct line to divine guidance. Prayer is where we take our findings from self-reflection and journaling and lay them before God, asking Him to illuminate our understanding and give us the strength to change. It's also where we seek the peace that transcends all understanding, which can guard our hearts and minds from future toxic intrusions. When you identify a trigger, bring it to God in prayer. Ask Him not only for relief but also for insight. Why does this particular thing bother you so much? What might He be trying to teach you through your reaction to it? You may not always get answers on the spot; it's about opening a dialogue with the Creator, who knows you better than you know yourself.

Finally, developing a personal action plan is where the rubber meets the road. This plan is your strategy for dealing with triggers as they arise. It draws on everything you've learned through self-reflection, journaling, and prayer. For each trigger, devise a plan. If, for example, you've discovered that social media is a significant trigger, your plan might involve setting specific times when you will and won't engage with social media or perhaps curating your feed to include only content that uplifts and encourages you. If certain relationships consistently lead to toxic thinking, your plan might consist of setting boundaries or planning responses ahead of time. Whatever the plan, the goal is the same: to reduce the power of triggers to disrupt your mental and spiritual health.

Remember, no one gets it perfectly right from the start in this ongoing process. It's about progress, not perfection. Each step in identifying, understanding, and managing your triggers is a step toward greater freedom and more profound peace. So, keep at it, knowing that each little victory is reshaping your mind, strengthening your faith, and bringing you closer to the abundant life God promises.

1.6 TOXIC THOUGHT PATTERNS VS. THE TRUTH OF SCRIPTURE: A COMPARATIVE STUDY

Embarking on the journey between the whispers of doubt and the profound truths found in Scripture is akin to navigating a spiritual battleground. This scenario might remind you of a classic depiction: an angel on one shoulder and a devil on the other, each fiercely competing for influence. In this modern iteration, however, it's not the devil we contend with but rather the insidious voices of toxic thoughts influenced by his agenda, sowing seeds of fear and uncertainty. According to Newton's Law of Inertia, an object will remain at rest or in uniform motion unless acted upon by an external force. Similarly, our minds will continue to be swayed by toxic thoughts unless counteracted by the transformative, powerful force of God's words. As we delve into this spiritual confrontation, we must rely on the Scriptures to provide the necessary force to change our trajectory, dismantling lies and offering strength and reassurance.

Understanding scripture isn't just about reading; it's about grasping the context, the intent, and the divine promise woven through them. Take, for instance, Psalm 34:18, "The Lord is close to the brokenhearted and saves those who are crushed in spirit." Written by David during a time of acute distress and danger, this Psalm is a vibrant testament to finding refuge in God's presence. It speaks to those feeling broken by life's betrayals and bruises, offering both company and deliverance.

The empowerment found in the scriptures is not just theoretical. It's as real as the ground under your feet, proven time and again in the lives of countless believers. Consider the story of Joseph, sold into slavery by his brothers, falsely accused, and imprisoned. Throughout his ordeal, Joseph could have succumbed to despair and bitterness. Imagine how many toxic thoughts he had to overcome! Thoughts about being victimized, being mistreated, having the wrong end of the stick, life being unfair to him, we can go on. Instead, he clung to the truths of God's sovereignty and goodness, eventually seeing God's purpose unfold in saving many lives through his position in Egypt. His story, found in Genesis 37-50, is a powerful reminder that our current struggles are not our final chapter. My friend, God is not done with you yet.

So, how can we apply these truths in the throes of toxic thinking? Start with scripture memorization. It's not just for Sunday School; it's your spiritual swordplay. Write down truths on cards, keep them on your phone, post them on your fridge—anywhere you might need a quick reminder. Then, practice what I like to call "scriptural replacement therapy." Each time a toxic thought surfaces, counter it with a truth. Speak it, think it, believe it. It's not about denying your feelings but anchoring them in something steadfast.

And for those times when the battle feels too intense, create a truth journal. Document every instance where a scriptural truth challenged a toxic thought and note the outcome. Over time, this journal will become a testament to your journey, a record of battles fought and victories won through the power of God's Word.

As we wrap up this exploration of lies versus truths, remember that this isn't about ignoring the complexities of our thoughts or the realities of our struggles. It's about standing on the solid ground of God's truth, allowing it to reshape our thinking, heal our hearts, and empower our lives. So the next time those toxic thoughts try to stage a takeover, remind yourself of who's really in charge. You're more than equipped for the battle with Scripture as your sword and shield. You are destined to win.

CHAPTER 2 BRAIN MAKEOVER - GROUNDING IN TRUTH

"Neuroscience has shown us that our thoughts and beliefs can physically alter our brain's structure—this is called neuroplasticity."

Have you ever wondered if what you believe could actually rewire your brain? Not just in a metaphorical "feel-good" kind of way, but in a real, measurable, scientific manner? Well, buckle up because we're about to dive into how your faith isn't just shaping your spirit—it's sculpting your brain, too! It's like discovering that eating your favorite chocolate could magically make you fit—it sounds too good to be true, but oh, how wonderful it is when it is true!

2.1 THE NEUROSCIENCE OF BELIEF: HOW FAITH SHAPES YOUR BRAIN

How Belief Rewires Our Brain Chemistry

Let's start with a bit of brainy talk. Neuroscience has shown us that our thoughts and beliefs can physically alter our brain's structure—this is called neuroplasticity. Now, throw faith into this mix; you've got a brain-changing powerhouse. When you engage in spiritual practices, whether prayer, meditation or just soaking in the truths of Scripture, you're not just passing time; you're paving neural pathways! Studies have indicated that regular spiritual mind-engaging activities can change the parts of the brain associated with attention, self-awareness, and emotion regulation. In this case, faith is the brain's personal trainer, helping bulk up the areas contributing to a healthier, happier you.

But how does this happen? When you believe in something greater than yourself—something as profound as the truths found in Christianity—your brain takes notice. For instance, engaging in prayer or spiritual meditation has been shown to decrease activity in the "default mode network," the part of the brain often associated with anxiety, depression, and self-focused thinking. What's essentially happening is that your brain is getting a clear signal to shift its focus from internal worries to a greater narrative to a bigger picture that involves a higher power and a broader purpose. This shift isn't just spiritually uplifting; it's neurologically beneficial, making your brain a more efficient and resilient organ.

Faith's Positive Effects on Mental Health

Exploring faith's serene and uplifting impact on our mental state reveals a fascinating picture. Numerous studies have linked regular spiritual practice with lower levels of stress and anxiety. Each prayer is a mini spa session for your brain, alleviating stress and bathing your neurons in soothing neurotransmitters. Yet, the benefits extend far beyond mere stress reduction. Such practices are potent tools for enhancing emotional health, paving the way to a deeper sense of peace and a more fulfilling experience of life satisfaction. Think of it as equipping your mental toolkit with an all-access pass to peace, resilience, and, yes, even joy.

Isaiah 26:3 states, "You will keep in perfect peace those whose minds are steadfast because they trust in you." This verse highlights the connection between steadfast faith in God and mental peace. Trusting in God, which requires faith, provides stability and tranquility, greatly enhancing mental health by reducing stress and fostering a sense of security.

Biblical Teachings and Brain Health

Connecting the dots between biblical teachings and brain health is fascinating. Take, for example, the practice of meditating on Scripture. This spiritual exercise is also a cognitive workout. When you meditate on biblical truths, you engage multiple areas of your brain. The memory areas get a jog, recalling the verses and their meanings. The understanding and reflection areas go on a sprint, diving deeper into the implications of these truths. And let's not forget the impact on the amygdala (our emotional processor), which gets a nice, calming pat on the back, reassuring it that all is well because you are in God's hands.

Practical Faith-Based Activities to Boost Brain Health

So, how can you put this into practice? Here are a few brain-boosting, faith-filled activities to try:

1. Scripture Meditation: Choose a verse each week to focus on. Spend a few minutes each day quietly reflecting on its meaning and relevance to your life. Meditation helps you

memorize scripture and embeds it into your cognitive processes.

2. Prayer Walks: Combine physical exercise with spiritual practice by taking prayer walks. As you walk, pray about what you see, feel, and hear. This gives you the benefits of exercise and helps keep your focus outward and upward.

3. Journaling: After reading a passage of Scripture, write down your thoughts, feelings, and any revelations that come to mind. This helps in reinforcing the neural pathways related to learning and memory.

4. Group Bible Study: Engaging in group discussions about faith can stimulate an array of cognitive functions, from language processing to complex reasoning. Plus, it's a great way to build social connections, which are crucial for mental health.

By integrating these practices into your life, you're not just nurturing your spiritual self; you're also giving your brain a boost. It's like hitting two birds with one divine stone—you grow in faith, and your brain reaps the benefits. So next time you pick up your Bible or fold your hands to pray, remember you're doing much more than it seems—you're training your brain to embrace a fuller, more prosperous, and more resilient life. And in this beautifully complex interplay between faith and neuroscience, we find yet another reason to marvel at the intricacies of how wonderfully we were made and just how marvelous God is.

2.2 SCRIPTURAL ANCHORS: VERSES THAT COMBAT COMMON LIES

Imagine having a treasure chest filled not with gold or jewels but with powerful words that have the divine power to uplift, heal, and transform you. That's what scripture can be in our lives, especially when wrestling with mental giants like fear, inadequacy, or despair. These verses aren't just ancient texts; they're alive, active, and incredibly relevant to our daily struggles. Let's dig into this treasure trove and discover critical verses that can become your go-to sources of strength and truth.

Integrating these verses into your daily life can transform them from words on a page to a vibrant, living dialogue with God. Start by choosing a verse that resonates with your current challenge. Write it out—yes, with a good old pen and paper because writing can help cement it in your memory. Carry it with you, or post it somewhere you'll see it throughout the day. Each time you read it, say it out loud. There's power in hearing the truth spoken in your voice.

But don't stop there. Make these verses a foundation for your prayers. When you talk to God, weave the scripture into your conversations. If you've chosen Isaiah 41:10 to combat fear, your prayer might look something like this: "Lord, you say not to fear because you are with me. I feel this fear creeping in, but I hold onto your promise that you will strengthen and uphold me. Help me to feel your presence right now." This practice turns scripture from a static reading into a dynamic, living interaction with your Creator.

Finally, personalize your scripture reflection. This isn't about adopting a one-size-fits-all approach but finding what speaks to your heart, struggles, and journey. Start a reflection journal where you write down the verses and your thoughts and feelings about them. How do they challenge you? Comfort you? What new insights do they bring? This practice deepens your relationship with scripture and with God, turning your moments of reflection into stepping stones toward greater spiritual and mental resilience.

By anchoring yourself in these truths, you're not just surviving but thriving. You're not just going through the motions but growing through them. And in this growth, you find solace and strength—not just for today, but for all the days to come.

2.3 MENTAL WELLNESS AND THE FRUIT OF THE SPIRIT

So, is there a hidden formula for maintaining mental wellness? Well, far from being a hidden secret, the blueprint for mental wellness is openly revealed in Galatians 5:22-23 through Paul's enumeration of the Fruit of the Spirit. Envision these fruits as vital nutrients for your soul, each uniquely contributing to your emotional health, mental clarity, and the deepening of your relationships. Let's explore the transformative qualities of these spiritual nutrients.

Love

In this bunch of fruits, love reigns supreme, inviting us to embrace others with selflessness and the compassionate heart of Christ. By nurturing love, we welcome it into our lives and freely extend it to others—this act of giving and receiving fosters an emotional cycle that diminishes the shadows of loneliness and separation.

Joy

Following closely to love is joy, like a beacon of light for the soul. This joy transcends mere happiness triggered by favorable circumstances; it roots itself in the serene assurance that, amidst life's chaos, God's sovereign hand is at work.

Peace

Peace then emerges, serving as our sanctuary amid our minds' tempests. Cultivating peace prevents the turmoil of the world from unsettling our inner calm. Envision a life where the irritations of daily inconveniences, like traffic delays or lengthy queues, lose their power to disturb your tranquility. Such is the essence of peace.

Patience

Following peace, patience is the enduring fruit, teaching us to persevere through challenges, even when surrender seems like the only option. It's about embracing the journey, anchored in the faith that God's perfect timing will unveil the best outcomes.

Kindness

A radiant jewel among the fruits invites us to extend grace and goodness to those around us—even those who may seem undeserving. It could be as simple as offering a warm smile to a cashier weighed down by the day's pressures or surprising a coworker with a coffee on a challenging day. These gestures of kindness do more than illuminate the days of others; they also ignite a symphony of positive hormones within us, such as dopamine and serotonin, enhancing our sense of happiness and well-being.

Goodness

Closely connected to kindness, goodness guides us toward a life of integrity, encouraging us to make decisions that stand out for moral clarity. It challenges us to follow the higher road, avoiding the temptation of easy shortcuts and ethical compromises. Embracing goodness fills us with a deep sense of pride and fulfillment, reinforcing our commitment to live in a way that mirrors our values and convictions.

Together, kindness and goodness weave a tapestry of actions and decisions that uplift our path and shine the light of Christ's love on those we meet.

Faithfulness

Faithfulness is about loyalty and dependability. It's being someone others can count on, and in doing so, we find a sense of purpose and belonging.

Gentleness

Often underrated is power under control. It's the soft answer that turns away wrath, the gentle nudge that guides without pushing.

Self-Control

Finally, self-control is the guardrail that keeps all the other fruits on track. It's about managing our impulses and emotions and making choices that align with our long-term goals rather than momentary desires.

Now, how do these fruits relate to mental health? Each one plays a unique role in fortifying our emotional and relational well-being. Love combats isolation, joy overcomes despair, peace silences anxiety, patience eases frustration, kindness soothes bitterness, goodness defends against guilt, faithfulness builds trust, gentleness calms conflict, and self-control prevents destructive behaviors. Each fruit is designed to counteract the struggles that often plague our minds.

But how do we cultivate these fruits? It starts with intentionality. Begin each day by asking God to fill you with His Spirit. Choose one fruit to focus on each week. If it's kindness, look for opportunities to be kind. If it's self-control, be mindful of your impulses. Keep a journal of your experiences. Write about challenges and victories. Reflect on how your focus on the Spirit's fruit is reshaping your thoughts and actions.

Engaging in the community is also crucial. These fruits grow best in the company of others striving to cultivate them too. Join a small group at church, or start a Bible study focused on the Fruit of the Spirit. Discuss each fruit, share insights, and encourage one another. As you practice these virtues together, you'll strengthen not only your spiritual walk but also the bonds within your community.

Remember, the growth of these fruits is a gradual process. Just like natural fruit need time to ripen, the Fruits of the Spirit develop through continuous, daily nurturing. So be patient with yourself. Celebrate small victories. Keep sowing seeds of spiritual discipline; in time, you'll reap a harvest of mental wellness and relational richness that will nourish you and those around you. And as you walk this path, remember, you're not just working on your mental health; you're cultivating a life that reflects the beauty and abundance of God's Spirit within you.

2.4 THERAPY WITH GOD - THE ROLE OF PRAYER IN MENTAL TRANSFORMATION

Consider prayer not merely as a spiritual obligation or a list of requests to God but as a powerful instrument for mental and emotional transformation. Envision prayer as an intimate conversation with a therapist (God) who already comprehensively understands you before you even speak. God tells us in Matthew 6:8, "Your Father knows what you need before you ask him." In the following verses, He tells us to pray for our needs, and in 1 Thessalonians 5:17, God commands us to pray continually. This perspective opens us to the true essence of prayer: it's not solely about altering our external situations but about transforming our inner selves—molding our thoughts, calming our emotions, and reshaping our neural pathways. God seeks to transform your whole life, inside and out!

Therapeutic Aspects of Prayer

Think about how you feel when you're stressed. Your heart races, muscles tighten, and your mind spins into overdrive. Now, picture yourself stepping into a serene prayer space amidst this chaos. A profound shift begins as you voice your concerns and realign your focus with God's promises. Your breathing becomes calm, your body relaxes, and your mind settles into peace. Scientifically, prayer has been shown to trigger the release of neurotransmitters like dopamine and serotonin, enhancing your mood and altering your perception for the better. Spiritually, it's as if you're handing over the heavy burdens you've been carrying to God, who holds them with ease. Prayer brings tranquility and transforms your perspective from confusion to clarity, from worry to confidence.

Biblical Examples of Transformative Prayer

The scripture is rich with narratives of transformation through prayer, illustrating its profound impact on personal trials. Consider Hannah, whose deep anguish over being childless drove her to pour her soul into the Lord in a raw, vulnerable prayer (1 Samuel 1:10-16). Her genuine plea and subsequent divine response blessed her with Samuel and instilled a profound peace within her once restless heart. Similarly, Daniel's unwavering dedication to prayer, even under the looming threat of execution, showcases the serenity and protection prayer provided him, especially visible when he faced the lions' den (Daniel 6:10). These accounts are more than historical events; they serve as powerful testimonials to the transforming power of prayer. When we lay our burdens before God, He doesn't just listen; He acts, changes, and revitalizes us.

Different Forms of Prayer for Various Needs

Prayer isn't one-size-fits-all; it's wonderfully versatile. Supplication, or asking God for help, is just one facet. There's also thanksgiving, where you focus on what God has done, which can be a powerful antidote to anxiety and negativity. Just try it. Start listing the things you're thankful for, and watch how your perspective shifts from what's wrong to what's right. Then there's contemplative prayer, a deep, meditative practice where you reflect on God's word or attributes, allowing the Holy Spirit to speak and minister to your heart. This form of prayer is like spiritual deep breathing, excellent for those moments when you feel overwhelmed and need to center your mind on God's presence.

Building a Routine of Daily Prayer

Integrating prayer into your daily routine may initially appear challenging; however, it fundamentally involves cultivating a habit gradually through consistent, incremental actions. Start with setting a specific time and place each day to pray, creating a routine that signals to your mind, "This is God's time." Morning can be great for offering your day up to God and aligning your heart with His. Evening can be a time to reflect, thank, and seek peace before sleep. If you commute, use that time to pray for your day, your family, or anything else on your heart. You can pray out loud, write your prayers in a journal, or say them silently; the method isn't as important as the commitment to consistently connect with God.

As you make prayer a non-negotiable part of your day, you'll find that it becomes as natural as breathing. You'll start to notice changes—not just in your circumstances, but in you. Worries that once loomed large seem manageable. Challenges that seemed impossible become opportunities to see God work. Your mind, once a battleground of anxiety and fear, becomes a garden of peace and trust. This transformation doesn't happen overnight, but with each prayer, you invite God to renew your mind, restore your spirit, and reshape your life. So, keep at it, knowing that each moment spent in prayer is a step toward a more peaceful, purposeful, and powerful life.

2.5 CULTIVATING A MINDSET OF GRACE AND FORGIVENESS

Unforgiveness entangles us in its intricate webs, much like holding onto a burning coal with the intention of throwing it at someone else—only to find that we are getting burned. This festering bitterness covertly takes root in our hearts, and before we know it, it's throwing block parties that invite stress, anxiety, and a host of mental and physical health issues. Let's dismantle this burden of resentment and replace it with the soothing balm of grace.

Reflect momentarily on the sensations you experience when you struggle to release a grudge. Perhaps you've felt a constricting sensation in your chest, shoulder tension, headaches, or an upset stomach. These symptoms are not merely physical discomforts but manifestations of unforgiveness burdening your body and mind. Psychologically, harboring resentment can perpetuate chronic stress, detrimentally affecting our overall well-being. It keeps our bodies in a constant fight or flight mode, with increased heart rate, tightened muscles, and elusive sleep. Such an environment becomes a breeding ground for anxiety, flourishing in the absence of peace. Persisting in this state can escalate to a myriad of health issues, including but not limited to depression, heart disease, and even memory issues. The hidden costs of holding onto unforgiveness are indeed profound and far-reaching.

Grace then becomes our beacon of hope. Within the Christian faith, grace gives favor and kindness to ourselves and others, even when it's not deserved. This concept reflects how God treats us, showering us with His endless love and forgiveness, no matter how many times we stumble. Living out this divine example can dramatically shift how we see ourselves and interact with those around us. Through the lens of grace, we start to see our imperfections and the faults of others in a new light, sparking profound change. We become more patient and understanding, not just with ourselves but everyone around us. Suddenly, a friend's lateness isn't an intentional offense but possibly a reflection of their battles. Similarly, we learn to separate our worth from our mistakes.

Practicing forgiveness isn't about denying your feelings or pretending everything is fine. It's about acknowledging the hurt and choosing to let it go, not for the offender's sake, but for your peace of mind.

Here's a step-by-step guide to start you off:

First, recognize the hurt. Be honest about how you feel and why. This isn't the time for sweeping under the rug; it's the time for a good, deep clean. Next, decide to forgive. It's a choice, often a hard one, but also a powerful one. Then, understand the offender's humanity. This can be tough, but try to see the situation from their perspective. What battles might they be fighting that you know nothing about?

And here's where it gets supernatural: ask for God's help. Forgiving isn't just a mental exercise; it's a spiritual one. Praying for the strength to forgive and for the well-being of the person who hurt you can sometimes feel like trying to benchpress a truck, but it's also where the heavy lifting happens in healing. Finally, let it go. This might be a one-time deal or a choice you have to make over and over again. Either way, whenever you choose forgiveness over bitterness, you take back your mental and spiritual real estate.

To cement this new mindset, try incorporating daily affirmations and prayers that focus on grace and forgiveness. Start your day by affirming, "Today, I choose forgiveness and peace over bitterness and strife." End your day with a prayer asking God to help you see where you can extend more grace to yourself and others. These practices aren't just good for your soul; they're like a spa treatment for your brain.

By embracing grace and forgiveness as core values, you enhance your mental well-being and lay the foundation for more meaningful and healthy relationships. In doing so, you cultivate an atmosphere ripe for peace—a place we all yearn to live every day. So, it's time to retire our grudge-holding habits and adopt a more graceful demeanor. Life is far too precious to spend it in the prison of unforgiveness.

As we wrap up this chapter on cultivating a mindset of grace and forgiveness, remember the profound impact that letting go of bitterness and embracing grace can have on your life. It frees you from the toxic chains of unforgiveness and aligns you more closely with God's heart, which is all about redemption and renewal. By choosing to forgive, you open space in your heart and mind for more joy, peace, and love—the essence of a well-lived life.

And as we turn the page to the next chapter, remember that each step you take in forgiveness is a step towards a freer, more joyful you. Let's continue exploring how we can grow in faith and love, transforming not just our minds but our entire lives.

CHAPTER 3 OVERCOMING STRESS AND ANXIETY WITH FAITH AND SCIENCE

"And the peace of God, which transcends all understanding, will guard your hearts and your minds in Christ Jesus."

— PHILIPPIANS 4:7

Have you ever felt like your mind is a bustling circus filled with tightrope walkers, jugglers, clowns, and even the occasional fire-breather? This chaotic performance is the work of stress, and frankly, it's not deserving of any accolades. However, imagine if your faith and scientific insight could transform this wild circus into a tranquil garden. Indeed, it's achievable. This chapter serves as your guide to converting the tumult of stress into moments of serene, faith-driven tranquility.

3.1 UNDERSTANDING THE SCIENCE OF STRESS AND THE PEACE OF FAITH

Exploring the Impact of Stress on Your Body

Let's talk about what's happening in your body when stress enters stage left. Imagine you're moments away from delivering a crucial presentation. Your heart races, your palms become damp, and your stomach feels as though it's hosting butterflies on steroids. This reaction is due to your body releasing cortisol and adrenaline, the stress hormones that act as an alert system, priming you for the 'fight or flight' response to imminent threats. While these hormones are lifesavers in situations of actual danger, they're less helpful when the 'threat' is an overflowing email inbox. The real issue arises when these hormones linger in your system for extended periods. The consequences include elevated blood pressure, a compromised immune system, and even alterations in brain functions, such as memory impairment. These are certainly not the conditions one would choose for their daily existence.

Theological Perspective on Peace

Transitioning to the biblical understanding of peace, we delve into a realm where tranquility is not merely an absence of conflict but a profound, divine gift that defies human logic. When we consider Philippians 4:7, we find a reassuring and revolutionary promise: "And the peace of God, which transcends all understanding, will guard your hearts and your minds in Christ Jesus." This scripture introduces us to a peace that is not just felt but experienced deeply within the soul—a peace that envelops our hearts and minds, offering protection and serenity amidst life's tumult. This divine peace is not superficial or fleeting; it is a wellspring of comfort and assurance that flows from the heart of God Himself. It reassures us that, regardless of the external chaos, we are cradled in the hands of a God who is sovereign over every storm. It's a peace that stands as a testament to our faith, a spiritual fortress that shields us from the despair that can arise amid life's trials.

Moreover, this peace serves as a solid spiritual foundation, a cornerstone upon which we can build our lives. It does not negate the reality of our struggles but invites us to view them through the lens of God's eternal perspective. In doing so, we are anchored not by our strength but by the unshakeable certainty that God is in control. Through every high and low, joy and sorrow, this peace remains steadfast, guiding us through the fiercest storms of life with a grace that is both empowering and transformative.

Interplay Between Science and Spirituality

So, how do faith and science intertwine in the realm of stress management? Harmoniously and effectively. Scientific evidence has shown that spiritual practices such as prayer and meditation can significantly lower stress levels. These acts quiet the body's alarm signals, reducing that 'fight or flight' response and enhancing the 'rest and digest' system, thus promoting tranquility in the mind and body. It's like telling your internal circus manager to take a coffee break.

Furthermore, faith can influence how you perceive and react to stress. Believing that you're not alone in your struggles—that God is with you—can change your stress narrative from one of feeling isolated to one of supported endurance. This shift in perspective can alter your physiological stress response, making you more resilient to life's pressures.

Faith in Action

Consider the story of Tisha, a social worker who often found herself overwhelmed by the emotional weight of her job. By integrating prayer into her morning routine, she began each day by casting her cares on God (1 Peter 5:7), significantly lowering her stress throughout the day. Then there's Lisa, a teacher in a high-pressure school. She started incorporating short meditative scripture readings into her lunch breaks, focusing on verses about peace and God's presence. This practice refreshed her mentally and created a noticeable decrease in her physical stress symptoms, like headaches and muscle tension.

These real-life examples illustrate how blending scientific strategies with spiritual practices isn't just possible—it's profoundly transformative. By understanding the biological basics of stress and embracing the peace offered through faith, you can navigate life's stresses with endurance, grace, and peace. So, next time you feel the circus starting up, remember: you have the best ringmaster in the business—your faith, backed by science, ready to turn chaos into calm.

3.2 NEUROPLASTICITY AND RENEWING YOUR MIND THROUGH SCRIPTURE

Neuroplasticity: The Brain's Marvelous Malleability

Let's imagine your brain as a dance floor, where neurons dance to the beats of your thoughts and experiences. Neuroplasticity is the DJ that mixes the tracks, constantly changing the tunes based on new moves you learn. In simpler terms, neuroplasticity refers to your brain's ability to reorganize itself by forming new neural connections throughout life. So, every time you learn something new or think in a different way, your brain gets busy rewiring itself to accommodate this fresh knowledge or perspective. It's like your brain is an artist, and every thought you have is a stroke of paint on the canvas of your mind.

So why is this exciting? Because it means you're not stuck with the mental habits or attitudes you have today; you can literally change your mind at the most fundamental level. If stress has been your default dance genre, through neuroplasticity, you can switch the beat to peace and tranquility. It's all about training your brain to favor pathways that lead to healthier thoughts and emotions. Now that is good news!

Scriptural Calls to Mind Transformation

Let's bring a divine dimension into this dance of neurons. Romans 12:2 says, "Do not conform to the pattern of this world, but be transformed by the renewing of your mind." Here, Paul isn't just making a poetic suggestion; he's laying down a life-changing strategy that aligns beautifully with the concept of neuroplasticity. This scripture is an invitation to overhaul your mental playlist, to stop replaying the world's tunes of fear, insecurity, and negativity by shutting up the lies, and to start playing God's tracks of peace, confidence, and love by filling your mind with the truth.

This scriptural advice isn't just spiritually sound; it's neuroscientifically savvy. When you immerse yourself in the truth of God's Word and allow it to shape your thoughts, you're not just being spiritually uplifted; you're also forging new neural pathways that can transform how you experience life. Each scripture you meditate on, each divine truth you ponder, acts like a mental workout, strengthening the pathways that lead to a more resilient and renewed mind.

Practical Steps for Mind Renewal

So, how do you practically engage in this mental gym? First, identify the old tracks that need changing. What negative beliefs or toxic thought patterns are keeping you stressed and anxious? Write them down. Next, find scriptures that directly counter these lies. For example, if you feel unworthy, immerse yourself in Zephaniah 3:17, which declares how God rejoices over you with singing. You are worthy!

Now, get into a daily habit of meditating on these truths. Set aside a few minutes each day to quietly reflect on them, allowing them to sink deep into your consciousness. As you do this, you're not just passively reading words but actively rewiring your brain. You can also use prayer as a powerful tool to reinforce these new neural pathways. Talk to God about the changes you're making. Ask Him to solidify these truths in your heart and mind.

Modern Neuroscience and Ancient Biblical Wisdom

The beautiful alignment between modern neuroscience and ancient biblical wisdom provides a robust framework for managing stress and anxiety. Scientists and theologians may use different vocabularies but converge on this truth: the mind is designed with renewal capabilities. Studies in neuroplasticity support the biblical call to transform our minds, giving scientific backing to the spiritual practice of mind renewal. This harmony between faith and science adds a layer of credibility and depth to our understanding of how we can live more fulfilled and less stressed lives.

By embracing the scientific insights into neuroplasticity and the biblical instructions for mind renewal, you're equipped with a powerful dual approach to transform your mental health. Each scripture you ponder, each positive affirmation you repeat, fortifies your mental pathways toward peace and positivity. You become not only a follower of Christ but also a savvy architect of your brain, actively participating in the divine dance of mental transformation that God has choreographed for you.

3.3 STRESS-RELIEF TECHNIQUES SUPPORTED BY SCIENCE AND THE BIBLE

Evidence-Based Stress Reduction Techniques

Diving into our toolkit, let's uncover some stress-relief methods that rival the relaxation of a spa day without the associated costs.

Deep Breathing

To begin with, consider the power of deep breathing. This simple act functions as a stress response's "pause button." Deep breaths signal your brain to enter a calm state, communicating relaxation to your body. In moments of overwhelming stress, a deep breath can be your sanctuary, reducing cortisol, the primary stress hormone in your body.

Integrating Christian contemplation with deep breathing enhances its benefits. As you breathe deeply, focus on God's presence. Inhale the Holy Spirit's peace and exhale your worries, transforming this practice into a moment of spiritual connection and rejuvenation.

This combination of deep breathing and contemplation not only calms your body but also nurtures your soul, aligning physical relaxation with a deeper sense of God's presence. It's a holistic approach to managing stress while drawing closer to God.

Progressive Muscle Relaxation

Progressive Muscle Relaxation (PMR) is an intentionally methodical process designed to soothe and relax each part of your body systematically. This technique involves a conscious effort to tense each muscle group firmly (but without causing strain) for a few moments and then releasing the tension abruptly, allowing a wave of relaxation to wash over the muscle. This act of alternating tension and relaxation helps increase awareness of physical sensations associated with stress, helping you recognize and manage stress more effectively. Imagine the feeling of lifting a heavy weight with each muscle group and then setting it down gently, acknowledging the lightness that comes with release. It's like realizing you've been carrying a bag of bricks—the weight you've grown so accustomed to, you've forgotten it's there—until you finally set it down and experience the relief and lightness of being unburdened.

Integrating Christian contemplation with PMR can deepen the experience. As you tense and release each muscle group, use this time to focus on God's presence and His comforting power. Contemplate a scripture or simply be still in His presence, allowing His peace to fill you. Contemplate His promise in Matthew 11:28-30, "Come to me, all you who are weary and burdened, and I will give you rest. Take my yoke upon you and learn from me, for I am gentle and humble in heart, and you will find rest for your souls. For my yoke is easy and my burden is light."

This combination not only enhances physical relaxation but also nurtures spiritual well-being, creating a holistic practice that soothes the body and uplifts the soul. Through this integrated approach, you can experience profound relief and a deep sense of connection with God.

Biblical Meditation and Prayer

Imagine integrating deep breathing with meditation on Philippians 4:6-7 which says, "Do not be anxious about anything, but in every situation, by prayer and petition, with thanksgiving, present your requests to God. And the peace of God, which transcends all understanding, will guard your hearts and minds in Christ Jesus."

As you inhale, allow the peace from these verses to fill you, and as you exhale, cast all your anxieties onto Him.

During progressive muscle relaxation, with each muscle group you relax, pair it with a prayer, symbolically handing over your worries to God with every breath out. This process becomes a physical and spiritual act of surrendering your burdens.

Integrating Routine Practices

Making these techniques a part of your daily routine can seem daunting, but remember, even small changes can make a significant impact. Start small; incorporate five minutes of deep breathing into your morning routine. Use a break at work for a quick progressive muscle relaxation session, or end your day with guided imagery before sleep. The key is consistency. Over time, these small practices add up, and before you know it, they become a natural part of your stress management strategy, easily accessible whenever you feel the pressures of life piling up.

3.4 THE ART OF BIBLICAL SELF-TALK: CHANGING NARRATIVES GENTLY

Identifying Negative Self-Talk Patterns

Have you ever caught yourself in a mental rant, with thoughts like "I can't do anything right" or "This is typical of me to mess up"? You're not alone in this mental tug-of-war. Often, we are our own harshest critics, with a stream of self-talk that's more defeating than uplifting. Recognizing these patterns is like catching that sneaky voice that whispers nothing but discouragement. It's about tuning into your internal dialogue and noticing when it takes a negative turn. For many, this happens during times of stress or failure, when it's all too easy to let self-doubt take the microphone.

But here's the twist: once you catch these culprits of chaos, you can start to SHUT them UP! It begins with awareness. Keep a thought journal. Write down any negative self-talk you notice and what triggered it. Was it a mistake at work? A critical comment from a friend? Or an unrealistic expectation you set for yourself? Mapping out these patterns will make you aware of them and help you anticipate and prepare for these mental battles. It's like setting a mental alarm that says, "Hey, this is where I usually start beating myself up. Let's tune the playlist to something more uplifting."

Replacing with Biblical Truths

The Bible is not just a book; it's a collection of God-breathed affirmations. For every piece of negative self-talk, there's a scripture waiting to counter it with truth. Feeling unworthy? Flip the script with Isaiah 43:4, where God says, "You are precious in my eyes and honored, and I love you." Struggling with feeling weak or inadequate? Remember 2 Corinthians 12:9, "My grace is sufficient for you, for my power is made perfect in weakness."

Transforming your self-talk with scripture is like replacing junk food with superfoods. It's not just about stopping the bad but starting the good. Create scripture cards or set up digital reminders with verses that specifically address your typical areas of self-criticism. Place them where you'll see them—on your bathroom mirror, car dashboard, or phone wallpaper. Let these truths be the first words you see in the morning and the last ones you reflect on at night. They are your spiritual affirmations, powerful enough to dismantle lies and strong enough to build up truth in their place.

Role of Self-Talk in Shaping Belief and Behavior

The conversations we have with ourselves can dramatically shape our lives. Engaging in positive self-talk rooted in scripture is not just about feeling better in the moment—it's a foundational shift that can transform our beliefs and actions. Moving from a mindset of "I can't" to declaring, "I can do all things through Christ who strengthens me" (Philippians 4:13) is more than an emotional lift. It marks a significant shift in our core beliefs. By changing our inner dialogue from one of doubt to one of divine strength and endless potential, we start to see ourselves and our capabilities in a new light.

This shift in perspective doesn't just affect our self-view; it changes how we interact with the world. Viewing life through this lens turns challenges into opportunities and obstacles into lessons, all powered by the strength and wisdom that Christ promises us.

Adopting this transformed narrative significantly influences how you handle stress, manage disagreements, and chase your dreams. It's similar to resetting your inner guidance system. Instead of being routed towards a place of doubt, you find yourself on a path leading to a state of confidence. While the journey remains unchanged, the shift in your final destination is monumental. You embark on a transformative journey with each scripture you embrace and each truth you affirm. It's not merely about moving from one point to another; it's about evolving into the version of yourself that God has called you to be.

Daily Self-Talk Routine

Creating a daily routine of positive self-talk infused with scripture can turn what might feel like a chore into a rhythm of renewal. Start your day with a "Scripture shower." Let God's Word cleanse your mind just as you cleanse your body. Pick a verse each morning to meditate on. Say it out loud, write it down, or reflect on it during your commute. Make it as routine as brushing your teeth but as personal as your signature.

Consider using technology to your advantage. Set up daily scripture alerts on your phone or use a Bible app that allows you to select a daily verse. Personalize this practice. You may be a visual learner and respond best to scripture cards placed around your workspace or at home. Perhaps you're auditory, and listening to scripture-based affirmations is more effective. Tailor this routine to fit your lifestyle, but keep the core unchanged: daily doses of divine truth, spoken over your life to transform your mind, heart, and actions.

By embedding these practices into your daily life, you're fighting off negative thoughts and fostering a fertile ground for faith and truth to flourish. As you do, watch how your mind's landscape blossoms from a battleground of doubt to a garden of peace and empowerment.

3.5 THE ROLE OF NUTRITION IN MENTAL WELLNESS: WHAT THE BIBLE SAYS

The adage, "You are what you eat," might invoke images of turning into a giant broccoli or a walking, talking blueberry muffin. However, beneath this light-hearted metaphor lies a profound truth: our dietary choices deeply influence our physical and mental well-being. Interestingly, the Bible offers rich insights into the importance of nourishing both the body and the mind with the right foods. Let us explore how integrating modern nutritional science with ancient scriptural wisdom comprehensively enhances mental health.

Nutritional Science for Mental Health

Seeing how specific nutrients affect our brain chemistry and mood is fascinating. Omega-3 fatty acids, for example, are like the superheroes of the fat world. These fats are found abundantly in fish like salmon and in flaxseeds and are crucial for brain health by helping to reduce inflammation and promote better brain function, which can influence our mood and stress levels. Then there are lean proteins, found in chicken, turkey, and legumes, which provide amino acids—critical components in neurotransmitter production that play a significant role in mood regulation.

Let's not forget complex carbohydrates, the unsung heroes in whole grains, fruits, and vegetables. These carbs help maintain our blood sugar levels, preventing mood swings and keeping our energy stable. They're the calm, collected friends who keep you steady when life throws curveballs. When our diet is balanced with these nutritional powerhouses, our body has the tools to manage stress and anxiety more effectively, proving that there's a direct link between the gut and the brain, often called the gut-brain axis. Thus, we have one more compelling reason to prioritize a healthy diet.

Biblical Dietary Laws and Principles

Exploring the rich wisdom in the Bible, we uncover dietary insights of lasting significance. For example, the dietary laws in Leviticus emerge not as mere rules but as intentional directives designed to foster comprehensive health. These sacred writings promote a nourishing and beneficial diet, mirroring a godly insight into what our bodies require to reach optimal health—for example, the prohibition of consuming fat and blood. Leviticus 7:23-24, "Do not eat any of the fat of cattle, sheep, or goats. The fat of an animal found dead or torn by wild animals may be used for any other purpose, but you must not eat it." This directive mirrors contemporary dietary advice to limit the intake of animal fats, which are associated with heart disease and other health issues. Avoiding the consumption of fat and blood promotes cardiovascular health and reduces the risk of consuming harmful substances.

Similarly, the fasting practices illustrated in the Book of Daniel, especially the Daniel Fast, shed light on the spiritual and physical benefits of a plant-based diet. Opting for vegetables and water over the indulgent meals of the Babylonian court wasn't just an act of defiance; it was a testament to the belief in the link between dietary choices and their impact on both body and spirit. Daniel and his friends' experience—a marked improvement in health and wisdom following their fast—underscores the significance of a disciplined approach to eating.

This conscious decision to choose simple, nourishing foods over opulent fare speaks volumes about the biblical understanding of the symbiotic relationship between our eating habits and overall health. It's a vivid illustration of how our spiritual well-being and physical health are intertwined, encouraging us to view food not merely as sustenance but as a means to honor our bodies and, by extension, the Creator. Integrating these timeless principles into our lives can lead to a more disciplined, healthful approach to eating that benefits our mind, body, and spirit.

It's fascinating to see how these biblical diets emphasize whole foods, which mirrors modern scientific guidance to avoid processed foods high in sugars and unhealthy fats—foods that can exacerbate anxiety and depression. Integrating these age-old principles into our modern diet can lead to better physical health and a clearer, more peaceful mind.

Creating a Balanced Diet Plan

So, how do we take these biblical insights and scientific facts and whip up a diet plan that nourishes body, mind, and spirit? Start with the basics: plenty of fruits and vegetables, whole grains, lean proteins, and healthy fats. Think of each meal as a palette where you paint a picture of nutritional balance. For instance, a breakfast of oatmeal (complex carbs) topped with walnuts (healthy fats) and a side of Greek yogurt (lean protein) isn't just delicious; it's a trinity of mood-boosting goodness.

But it's not just about what you eat; it's about how you eat. The Bible often depicts meals as communal, reflective times. Emulating this, we can transform eating from a rushed chore into a conscious practice. Share meals with others when possible, and take a moment to express gratitude for the food and the nutrition your body will enjoy, a practice that can enrich your spiritual and emotional well-being.

3.6 THE ROLE OF FASTING IN MENTAL CLARITY AND RENEWAL

Imagine hitting the reset button on your mental and spiritual health. That's a bit like what fasting does; it's not just about skipping meals; it's about gaining more clarity, spiritual depth, and, surprisingly, more peace. When you fast, you're stepping back from the daily grind to focus more on your relationship with God, allowing your body and mind to detox from life's constant demands. Think of it as a time for cleansing and revitalizing your soul.

Exploring the Spiritual and Psychological Benefits of Fasting

Scientifically, fasting is shown to promote mental clarity. When you fast, your body shifts from using glucose to ketones as its primary energy source, a state that some studies suggest can lead to a clearer mind. But the benefits aren't just about clearer thinking; they're deeply spiritual. Fasting can heighten your spiritual sensitivity, making you more attuned to God's voice and more reflective of His word. It's as if you're tuning out the world's noise to tune into divine frequencies.

In the scriptures, fasting is consistently associated with seeking a more profound connection with God and discerning His guidance. This spiritual practice is exemplified in the story of Esther, who, before making a pivotal decision that would save her people, proclaimed a fast among the Jews. This act of fasting was not just a plea for divine intervention but also a communal submission to God's will, demonstrating faith and dependence on His providence.

Similarly, Jesus' 40 days of fasting in the wilderness, preceding His public ministry, illustrate the importance of thoroughly preparing one's heart and mind to embrace God's plan. During this time, Jesus faced temptations but emerged victorious, fortified by His communion with the Father. These significant periods of fasting were not merely ceremonial; they were transformative experiences that led to monumental spiritual revelations and decisions, ultimately altering the course of history and destiny.

Health-wise, fasting has numerous benefits. It can improve metabolic health by reducing insulin resistance, promoting better blood sugar control, and lowering inflammation. Additionally, fasting triggers autophagy, a cellular cleanup process that removes damaged cells and regenerates new ones, contributing to overall health and longevity. These physical benefits complement the mental and spiritual clarity gained during fasting, creating a holistic approach to well-being.

A Guide to Different Types of Fasts

Fasting doesn't always mean abstaining from all food and drink; there are several ways to engage in this spiritual discipline, each serving different purposes. A full fast typically involves abstaining from all food and drinking only liquids like water or juice, and it is often used for short periods when seeking serious spiritual renewal. Then there's the partial fast, which might involve giving up particular types of food—like meats and sweets—as seen in the Daniel Fast, which focuses on fruits, vegetables, and whole grains.

Choosing your type of fast should align with your physical capabilities and spiritual goals. For instance, a day or two of juice fasting might be appropriate if you're looking for general spiritual refreshment or guidance on a specific issue. If you're seeking profound spiritual renewal or have a significant decision to make, a longer partial fast, like the Daniel Fast, could be more suitable. Always ensure your fast is tailored to what you can handle physically and what you seek spiritually.

Tips for Safe and Effective Fasting

Fasting, while beneficial, needs to be approached with wisdom. You may need to consult a healthcare provider, especially if you have health conditions like diabetes or heart disease. Staying hydrated during a fast is crucial, so keep water on hand and sip throughout the day. Ease into and out of your fast. Begin reducing your food intake a few days before your fast, and reintroduce foods gently afterward, starting with something light like broth or salad to avoid shocking your system.

Listen to your body while fasting. If you experience severe symptoms like dizziness, confusion, or extreme weakness, you must reconsider your approach. Fasting is meant to be challenging, but it shouldn't be harmful.

Integrating Prayer and Meditation with Fasting

The true power of fasting is unlocked when combined with prayer and meditation. The mental clarity that comes from fasting can provide a more focused time of prayer and reflection. Use this time to delve deeper into scripture or spend prolonged periods in prayer. Again, keep a journal during your fast to record insights and revelations. This can be particularly enriching, as you may notice more profound spiritual understanding or answers to prayers during this time.

Consider also the practice of 'prayer walking' while fasting. In this practice, you take to a quiet path or park, allowing the physical activity to complement your spiritual exercise. Prayer walking can enhance the sense of connecting with God through His creation, helping to ground your spiritual experience in the physical world.

When done responsibly and thoughtfully, fasting can be a powerful tool for renewing both mind and spirit. It offers a unique blend of physical discipline and spiritual insight, providing a pathway to deeper faith and clearer thinking. As you embark on this practice, remember it's not about what you're giving up but what you stand to gain—a refreshed body, a renewed mind, and a rejuvenated spirit.

3.7 TAKING CARE OF GOD'S TEMPLE: PHYSICAL WELLNESS FOR MENTAL HEALTH

Have you ever considered that your workout could be as spiritually uplifting as your worship? If we frame it right, breaking a sweat can be a form of praise. When we talk about taking care of our bodies, it's not just about avoiding that extra slice of cake; it's about honoring the incredible gift God has given us. Our bodies are described in 1 Corinthians 6:19-20 as temples of the Holy Spirit, and just like any temple, they require upkeep—not just for aesthetics, but for function, especially when it comes to managing our mental health.

Let's explore how consistent physical activity can be a continuous source of blessings for our mental well-being. Exercise is a powerhouse when it comes to combating anxiety and depression, and it's all thanks to those little internal cheerleaders known as endorphins. These are the body's natural stress-fighters and mood-lifters. Imagine them as your body's naturally brewed cup of coffee, perking you up, not with a temporary caffeine buzz, but with a lasting boost to your mood. When you exercise, your body releases these endorphins, leading to the 'runner's high.' But the benefits aren't just about feeling good in the moment; they extend to a more resilient, joy-filled you, capable of tackling stressors with a more substantial, steadier hand.

But here's where it gets even more beautiful. When we view exercise as a form of worship, each step, each lift, each lap becomes an act of reverence, a way of thanking God for the body we've been blessed with. Afterall, it is in Him that we live and move and have our being (Acts 17:28).

This perspective transforms routine workouts into acts of worship and gratitude. It's not just about keeping fit; think of it as expressing thanks with every fiber of our being. Integrating this mindset starts with setting intentions. Before you begin your exercise, take a moment to dedicate the session to God. You could say a quick prayer like, "Lord, thank you for the strength to move and the space to grow. Let this time strengthen my body and my connection with You."

Incorporating worshipful intentions into your exercise routine can be as simple as playing worship music while you run or meditating on scripture during your cool-down. Imagine you're on a peaceful jog in the park, and with each step, you're meditating on Isaiah 40:31, "But those who hope in the Lord will renew their strength. They will soar on wings like eagles; they will run and not grow weary; they will walk and not be faint." Suddenly, your run has transformed from physical activity to a spiritual reinforcement of your faith.

When we care for our bodies through exercise and see this care as a form of worship, we're not just maintaining physical health but enhancing our spiritual vitality. Every drop of sweat becomes a testament to our gratitude for life, and every breath, a prayer of thanksgiving. So, as you consider your next workout, remember that it's not just about the physical benefits. It's an opportunity to honor God with your body, turn what is routine into something sacred, and strengthen your muscles and your faith. In this holistic approach, every workout is a worship session, every stretch a prayer opportunity, and every run time to meditate, bringing you closer to God and the peace He promises.

3.8 SLEEP HYGIENE TIPS FROM PROVERBS AND PSALMS

Sleep is that serene haven where our bodies rejuvenate, our minds find peace, and ideally, no unexpected disturbances from children or pets occur in the wee hours! Beyond merely providing rest, a good night's sleep is a powerful ally for mental health. It acts as a reset button for our brains, erasing the day's stress and concerns. Let's explore the significance of sleep for our mental wellness and discover how scriptural wisdom can guide us toward more restful nights.

The Scientific Importance of Sleep

Sleep is crucial not just for feeling alert but for robust mental health. It plays a critical role in processing emotional information and helping us manage stress and anxiety. When we sleep, our brain goes on a nighttime mission – consolidating memories, processing emotions, and restoring itself. It's like the night shift comes in to tidy up the mess left by the day shift. Without enough sleep, we might be more irritable, unable to concentrate, and more susceptible to stress. Even more, chronic sleep deprivation can lead to severe mood swings and even depression, not to mention a whole host of physical health problems. It's clear that sleep isn't just a luxury; it's a must-have for maintaining our mental, emotional, and physical health.

Sleep Advice from Scripture

The scriptures are not silent about the blessings of rest. Proverbs 3:24 promises, "When you lie down, you will not be afraid; when you lie down, your sleep will be sweet." This promise isn't just a comforting thought; it's a directive for trust, letting us know that laying our worries at God's feet can lead to peaceful, fear-free rest. Then there's Psalm 4:8, which offers this tranquil assurance: "In peace, I will lie down and sleep, for you alone, Lord, make me dwell in safety." These verses highlight a profound truth: our sleep is a physical necessity and a spiritual gift. They teach us that proper rest comes from feeling secure in God's care.

Tips for Better Time in Bed

So, how can we turn these biblical insights into better sleep habits? First, establish a regular sleep schedule. Our bodies thrive on routine. Going to bed and waking up at the same time each day sets our internal clock to expect rest at certain times, making it easier to fall asleep and wake up naturally. Think of it as training your body to know when to shut down the factory for the night.

Creating a restful environment is also vital. This requires making your bedroom a sanctuary of calm. Invest in comfortable bedding, use soft, soothing colors, and keep the room cool and dark. Consider a bedtime ritual that helps you wind down, like reading

(Psalms are great for this), praying, or listening to soft music. This ritual tells your brain it's time to slow down and prepare for sleep.

Another tip? Watch what and when you eat and drink. Avoid heavy meals, caffeine, and alcohol close to bedtime. They can disrupt sleep and prevent you from falling into the deep, restorative stages of sleep you need. Instead, opt for a light snack if you're hungry, like yogurt or a banana, which won't sit like a rock in your stomach.

Remember that good sleep hygiene is a pillar of mental wellness, a gift from God worth investing in. By viewing our sleep routines through the lens of scripture and science, we enhance our nights and enrich our days, living out God's promise of peace and rest. So tonight, as you lay down, remember that God's Word offers spiritual insights and practical guidance for the sweet sleep your body and mind crave.

Next, we'll explore the importance of community in mental wellness, revealing how our connections with others can support and enhance our journey to better mental health. Stay tuned, and sweet dreams!

CHAPTER 4 BUILDING A SUPPORTIVE COMMUNITY

"And let us consider how we may spur one another on toward love and good deeds, not giving up meeting together, as some are in the habit of doing, but encouraging one another—and all the more as you see the Day approaching."

— *HEBREWS 10:24-25*

Have you ever felt lost in a personal wilderness, yearning for the warmth and joy of belonging? Isolation is a prevalent modern-day issue plaguing our society, exacerbating mental ill health. Envision transforming that barren personal landscape into a thriving oasis with abundant encouragement, love, and shared experiences. This scenario highlights the powerful impact a supportive community has on our spiritual and emotional wellness.

In a world where isolation can lead to heightened feelings of anxiety, depression, and loneliness, finding your tribe becomes essential. While it might seem like we are constantly in touch with others through social media, superficial interactions can lead to pronounced loneliness. Having people who empathize with your struggles and rejoice in your victories creates a sense of connection and belonging, which is especially important. Let's discuss how nurturing a solid community can profoundly uplift your mental and spiritual health journey, helping to counter the adverse effects of isolation and promoting a more holistic sense of well-being.

4.1 THE POWER OF FELLOWSHIP IN HEALING AND GROWTH

Healing Through Shared Experiences

The concept of 'sharing is caring' takes on a profound meaning when it comes to fellowship. There's something almost magical about opening up to a group that not only listens but truly hears you. It's like unloading burdens you've been toting around, thinking you must carry them solo. Within a fellowship, you discover that others have been trekking through similar challenging terrains. Sharing personal struggles and victories isn't just about getting things off your chest; it's therapeutic, like weaving a safety net of empathy and understanding that catches us when we fall.

This communal exchange of experiences can lighten our emotional loads and clarify our paths. Hearing how others navigated through their valleys provides practical insights and instills hope. It reminds us that healing isn't just a possibility; it's a journey that others are walking alongside us, step by step.

Scriptural Basis for Community

Reflecting on the early church as depicted in Acts 2:42-47, we see believers who went beyond mere meetings; they embodied shared living. Together, they broke bread, engaged in prayer, and generously shared their possessions with one another. This was not merely communal living out of necessity but a joyful demonstration of their unity and faith. They understood something profound—that proper growth and healing flourish not in solitude but within the nurturing embrace of community.

These scriptures aren't dusty old texts but blueprints for building robust communities today. They teach us that sharing our lives through fellowship isn't just a nice add-on to our spiritual routines; it's essential for solid faith and emotional resilience. It's about creating a space where hearts connect, burdens are halved, and joys are doubled.

Building Trust in Fellowship Groups

Find communities within your local church through small groups, women's fellowships, youth meetings, etc., where vulnerability is not just welcomed but safeguarded. It's not just about socializing; it's about intertwining our lives so that we all grow, heal, and thrive together. In a world that champions self-sufficiency, this reminds us of the profound truth that we were never meant to go it alone. The journey is easier and richer when we walk it together.

Moreover, there are even more profound spiritual benefits to not forsaking the gathering together of the saints. As the Bible says in Hebrews 10:24-25, "And let us consider how we may spur one another on toward love and good deeds, not giving up meeting together, as some are in the habit of doing, but encouraging one another—and all the more as you see the Day approaching." Therefore, if the prospect of engaging in group activities or cultivating closer relationships within your community appears intimidating, consider this understanding as encouragement. Welcome the complex elegance and profound restoration that unfolds through the experience of fellowship.

4.2 ESTABLISHING ACCOUNTABILITY PARTNERSHIPS WITHIN THE CHURCH

Imagine stepping into an environment as nurturing and comforting as your favorite coffee spot, where warm smiles welcome you and your unique preferences are known by heart. In this place, you feel valued and seen. This sense of community and connection reflects the essence of forming an accountability partnership within your church community. It's about connecting with someone who intimately knows your spiritual journey, empathizes with your challenges and triumphs, and supports you in maintaining a robust faith and a healthy life. This isn't just about having a spiritual buddy; it's about fostering a relationship that holds you gently yet firmly to your commitments, helping you navigate life's ups and downs while keeping your faith intact.

Accountability partnerships are like having a personal trainer for your soul. They help maintain spiritual discipline, which can be particularly crucial in times when our mental health might be wavering. These partnerships protect against isolation—a major factor that can exacerbate feelings of anxiety and depression. By regularly checking in with someone who cares about your spiritual well-being, you're less likely to fall into harmful patterns or secretive behaviors that can lead to spiritual and emotional crises. Think of it as preventative maintenance for your heart and soul, ensuring you stay aligned with your spiritual goals even when the going gets tough.

Choosing the right accountability partner is crucial—it's kind of like picking a dance partner. You want someone who can match your steps and shares similar values and spiritual goals. This person should be trustworthy, able to keep confidences, and committed to mutual growth. They should be someone you respect and whose insights you value, ideally someone who perhaps has walked a bit longer on their spiritual journey and can provide wisdom and guidance. It's also important that this person can challenge you when necessary—always in love—to help you grow and prevent you from stagnating or deviating from your path. This way you can carry each other's burdens according to Galatians 6:2.

The structure of an effective accountability relationship requires regular check-ins, honest communication, and mutual encouragement. Regular weekly or biweekly meetings help keep the relationship dynamic and responsive. These aren't just casual catch-ups but intentional times to discuss victories, struggles, and everything in between. Honesty is the currency of this relationship. It's about being open about where you're succeeding and where you're struggling without fear of judgment.

Encouragement plays a dual role; it's about cheering each other on and pushing one another toward deeper spiritual truths and practices. This structure ensures that the relationship is always moving forward, always edging closer to the shared goal of spiritual maturity.

Handling setbacks and challenges within this relationship is where its true strength is tested. It's inevitable that, at some point, one or both of you might stumble. Maybe it's a missed meeting or a spiritual misstep. Here, the focus should be on growth and forgiveness. Approach setbacks not as failures but as opportunities to extend grace and deepen understanding. Discuss openly what went wrong and why, and decide together how to better handle similar situations in the future. This approach strengthens the bond and models the kind of forgiveness and resilience we're called to exhibit as followers of Christ.

James 5:16 states, "Therefore confess your sins to each other and pray for each other so that you may be healed. The prayer of a righteous person is powerful and effective." By openly acknowledging our missteps and seeking mutual support, we foster an environment of accountability and healing. This scriptural principle underscores the value of transparency and mutual support within our relationships, further strengthening the community bond and promoting spiritual and emotional well-being.

In such a partnership, every challenge overcome and every setback navigated is a testament to the power of shared spiritual commitment. It's about having someone to share the load and double the joy. As you walk this path together, you'll find that your individual journeys are enriched, your burdens are lighter, and your spiritual growth is accelerated. So, consider establishing such a partnership in your church community. It could be the key to unlocking a deeper, more fulfilling spiritual life, ensuring you never have to walk alone.

4.3 MENTORSHIP: RECEIVING AND PROVIDING GUIDANCE

The role of a mentor in the Christian community can often be likened to that of a spiritual shepherd—someone who guides, protects, and nurtures the flock. In this relationship, the mentor provides wisdom, support, and practical advice from their journey with Christ. This guidance is crucial as it helps navigate the often turbulent waters of personal and spiritual growth. Meanwhile, the mentee brings to the table a willingness to learn, fresh perspectives, and, often, a rejuvenating energy that can inspire the mentor as well. This partnership fosters a dynamic where both individuals are encouraged to grow in faith, hold each other accountable, and deepen their understanding of God's word.

Finding the right mentor can sometimes feel like searching for a needle in a haystack, but it doesn't have to be daunting. Start by praying for guidance—ask God to lead you to someone who can provide the spiritual and emotional wisdom you seek. Keep an eye out in your church community—perhaps a leader whose teachings resonate with you or a fellow church member whose faith walk inspires you. Don't hesitate to ask your pastor for recommendations; they can often connect you with potential mentors with a heart for guiding others. Once you've found a potential mentor, invite them for a coffee or a meal. Use this time to discuss your spiritual goals and see if there's a mutual desire to embark on a mentorship journey together.

On the flip side, being a mentor is about more than having all the answers—it's about being willing to walk alongside someone as they explore their faith and life questions. Effective mentorship requires patience, empathy, and an authentic commitment to listening and sharing openly. If you feel called to mentor someone, start by evaluating your own journey. Are there experiences you've navigated that could help others? Spend time in prayer and scripture to ensure your guidance is rooted in biblical truth. It's also essential to be proactive—attend mentorship training sessions if your church offers them, and be open about your willingness to mentor within your community circles.

So whether you are seeking a mentor or stepping into the role of one, you are engaging in a sacred act of mutual edification, where the bonds formed and the growth experienced can have everlasting impacts. So, as you consider entering into a mentorship relationship, remember that you are stepping into a divine opportunity to provide and receive wisdom, encouragement, and spiritual nourishment. In this beautiful exchange, lives are transformed, faith is deepened, and God's work is done in ways that continually renew and inspire both the mentor and the mentee.

4.4 ENGAGING FAMILY IN YOUR JOURNEY TO MENTAL WELLNESS

Involving your family in your spiritual routines can be a delightful adventure. You could start with something as simple as morning devotions over breakfast, where each family member shares a verse or a prayer intention for the day. It's like passing around a basket of fresh spiritual fruits to nourish everyone for the day ahead. Or, consider establishing a weekly family worship night where you sing, pray, and dive into the Bible together. Make it engaging by incorporating interactive elements like Bible story re-enactments or scripture-based scavenger hunts for the little ones. These practices not only bring you closer to God but also to each other, reinforcing your spiritual bonds.

Communicating effectively about mental health within the family setting is crucial. It starts with openness and honesty. Set a time to sit down with your family and share your needs and experiences. Use simple, straightforward language to describe what you're going through and what kind of support you'd appreciate. For instance, you might explain that having quiet time after dinner helps you manage stress better or that you need their understanding when you feel overwhelmed. Encourage them to express their thoughts and needs, too. This transparent communication can help prevent misunderstandings and build a more robust, empathetic family unit.

The role of the family as a support system cannot be overstated. Families serve as a multifaceted support system—adaptable, strong, and profoundly encouraging when their strengths are effectively engaged. They can provide a unique type of accountability and encouragement different from what friends or church members offer. For instance, they're there to notice the small changes in your demeanor or daily habits that others might miss, which can be crucial in managing mental health. Encourage regular check-ins where each family member can share how they're doing and what they're struggling with without judgment. These moments can strengthen the ties that bind you, ensuring everyone feels valued and supported.

Navigating challenges within family dynamics, especially when it comes to mental health, requires patience and grace. Conflicts arise, perhaps from misunderstandings about mental health issues or from the stress that occasionally comes with deep emotional discussions. When these moments occur, focus on reconciliation and understanding. Approach each situation with a mindset of learning rather than blaming. Use conflicts as opportunities to explore deeper issues that may need addressing, whether it's setting healthier boundaries or seeking external support from counseling or pastoral care.

Integrating these strategies into your family life transforms your home into a stronghold of mutual support and spiritual growth. This doesn't mean that challenges won't arise, but with your family by your side, armed with understanding and faith, you'll find that navigating the path to mental wellness becomes a shared, significantly more manageable journey.

"These commandments that I give you today are to be on your hearts. Impress them on your children. Talk about them when you sit at home and when you walk along the road, when you lie down and when you get up."

— DEUTERONOMY 6:6-7

Remember, your family isn't just there for the holidays or special occasions; they are your day-to-day companions on the road to mental wellness. By fostering an environment of open communication, shared spiritual practices, and mutual support, you create a home where every member can flourish—spiritually, emotionally, and mentally.

INVITATION TO MAKE A DIFFERENCE

Help Others Overcome

"And they overcame him by the blood of the Lamb and by the word of their testimony..."

— REVELATIONS 12:11

When you share your story, you help others overcome their challenges. So, let's take a moment to spread some joy and make a real difference together.

I have a question for you...

Would you help someone you've never met, even if you never got credit for it?

Who is this person, you ask? They are like you. Or, at least, like you used to be. Someone who's searching for answers, wanting to grow, and needing a little guidance.

Our mission is to equip girls and women with truth and practical tools to overcome toxic thoughts trying to undermine their identity in Christ. Everything I do stems from that mission.

And, the only way to accomplish that mission is by reaching... well...everyone.

This is where you come in.

Most people do judge a book by its cover (and its reviews).

So here's my ask on behalf of a struggling woman you've never met: Please help her by leaving this book a review.

Your gift costs no money and less than 60 seconds to make real, but can change a fellow woman's life forever.

Your review could help...

...one more woman find peace in her thoughts.
...one more mother feel confident and loved.
...one more daughter embrace her true self.
...one more friend discover inner joy.
...one more dream come true.

To get that 'feel good' feeling and help this person for real, all you have to do is...and it takes less than 60 seconds... leave a review.

Simply scan the QR code to leave your review:

If you feel good about helping a faceless reader, you are my kind of person. Welcome to the club. You're one of us.

I'm excited to continue sharing tips on how you can conquer toxic thoughts and embrace life with transforming truths. You'll love the practical ideas I will share in the coming chapters.

Thank you from the bottom of my heart. Now, back to our brain makeovers. 😊

Your transformation partner, Mataila.

PS - Fun fact: It is more blessed to give than to receive. If you'd like to be a blessing to another woman - and you believe this book will help them - send a copy of this book their way.

CHAPTER 5 DAILY PRACTICES FOR A SOUND MIND

"The hand of the diligent will rule, while the lazy will be put to forced labor."

— *PROVERBS 12:24*

In this chapter, we'll explore how you can transform each morning into a chance to cultivate a positive mindset for the day ahead, guided and directed by God, not just as a companion but as the one steering your path.

5.1 STARTING YOUR DAY WITH GOD: MORNING ROUTINES TO SET A POSITIVE TONE

Importance of a Structured Morning Routine

Let's face it, mornings can feel like a battleground. From alarm clocks that seem to ring too early to the mad dash out the door, it's easy to feel like you're losing the day before it even starts. But here's a little secret: the first hour of your morning is golden. It's a pristine, untouched canvas upon which you can paint whatever tone you want for your day. Now, imagine starting each day without chaos but with a moment of peace and purpose.

Welcoming God into your morning routine is more than just a bonus; it's like tuning your heart before the day's symphony begins —it lays the groundwork for everything that follows. When you start your day focused on God, you anchor yourself in His presence, which can bring peace and perspective that permeates your entire day. It's about declaring that before you face the world, you face your Creator and draw your strength and inspiration from Him. As Psalm 5:3 says, "In the morning, Lord, you hear my voice; in the morning, I lay my requests before you and wait expectantly." This scripture highlights the importance of seeking God early in the day, setting a spiritual tone that can positively influence all your daily interactions and tasks.

Elements of a Spiritual Morning Routine

Now, what does a morning routine with God look like? It's as varied as the beautiful tapestry of believers worldwide, but here are a few key components you might consider:

- Prayer: Think of it as your morning chat with God. It doesn't have to be long or eloquent. Just open your heart to God about the day ahead. Ask for His guidance, thank Him for His blessings, and lay your concerns at His feet.
- Scripture Reading: Dive into God's Word. You could follow a Bible reading plan or simply open the Bible and read a passage. Let the scriptures fill your mind with divine wisdom and truth. If you're unsure where to start, the Psalms are packed with expressions of hope, trust, and

the steadfastness of God's love—perfect for setting a positive tone for the day.
- Worship Music: Let your morning shower double as a time of worship. Play a few worship songs as you prepare for the day. Sing along or let the music play in the background. It's a soul-lifting way to start the day.

Personalizing Your Morning Routine

The beauty of a morning routine is that it's deeply personal. What works for one person might not work for another, and that's okay. The key is to craft a routine that fits your lifestyle and resonates with your spiritual needs. Not a morning person? Start small—maybe with a five-minute prayer or a single worship song. Gradually, you can add more elements or extend the time as you find what works best for you.

If time is tight, consider audio Bibles or worship playlists you can listen to while multitasking in the morning. The goal is not to add stress but to infuse your morning with small acts of faith that prepare you for the day ahead.

Impact on Daily Outlook

The transformative power of beginning your day with God cannot be overstated. This simple act has the potential to alter your entire perspective. Suddenly, the traffic jam isn't a disaster; it's an opportunity to pray. The big meeting isn't a stressor; it's a chance to trust in God's ability to give you strategy and words to say during the meeting.

Remember, the Bible assures us that God can grant us ingenuity and wisdom. Exodus 35:31-32 says, "And He has filled him with the Spirit of God, with wisdom, with understanding, with knowledge and with all kinds of skills—to make artistic designs for work in gold, silver, and bronze." This scripture reminds us that God provides peace and strength and endows us with creativity and skill. By starting your day with Him, you open yourself up to His guidance and innovative solutions for the challenges the day will bring. This alignment with God's wisdom transforms ordinary moments into divine opportunities, enriching your daily life with His presence and ingenuity.

Imagine walking into your day charged not with anxiety but with anticipation for what God will do. It's like going from watching life in black and white to life in vibrant color. Everything is the same, yet nothing is the same because you've started your day by anchoring yourself to the steadfastness of God's love. So tomorrow, when the alarm goes off, remember that each morning is a new beginning, a fresh opportunity to set the tone for a day walked in faith and bathed in grace. Why not start it with God? After all, with Him, even the mundane can become miraculous.

5.2 SETTING BOUNDARIES: A GUIDE FOR PROTECTING MENTAL SPACE

Picture your mind as a treasured garden. Just as a garden needs a fence to protect it from unwelcome intruders and unintended harm, your mental space requires boundaries to thrive and bear fruit. Setting boundaries is not about shutting out the world; it's about creating an environment where your emotional and spiritual well-being can prosper. It's similar to installing an inviting yet sturdy gate to guard your personal sanctuary.

Importance of Boundaries for Mental Health

Why are boundaries so crucial? Without them, it's like leaving your garden gate wide open; anything and anyone can wander in and out at will. This can lead to a chaotic mental environment where stress and burnout are frequent visitors. Boundaries help you define what is and isn't allowed in your mental space. They help you prioritize your needs, manage your energy, and maintain peace. It's about knowing when to say yes and how to say no and feeling perfectly fine about both.

Boundaries are essential for maintaining mental wellness, especially in today's hyper-connected world, where demands on your time and attention can be incessant. They help you guard against the overload of information and expectations, which can lead to anxiety and stress. By setting clear boundaries, you're essentially teaching yourself and others how to treat your garden—what's allowed in, what isn't, and how best to nurture its growth.

Ephesians 6:17 advises us to "take the helmet of salvation and the sword of the Spirit, which is the word of God." The helmet of salvation symbolizes protecting your mind from negative influences and thoughts. Just as a physical helmet shields your head from injury, the helmet of salvation guards your thoughts and mental state, reinforcing your identity in Christ and His promises.

By combining the practical step of setting boundaries with the spiritual act of wearing your helmet of salvation, you create a robust defense against the pressures and demands of modern life. This dual approach helps maintain mental wellness by filtering out harmful influences and grounding you in the truth of God's Word. This balanced strategy nurtures your mental and spiritual health, enabling you to flourish in a world that often seeks to overwhelm and distract.

Biblical Basis for Boundaries

Interestingly, the concept of boundaries is deeply biblical. Scriptures provide numerous examples of boundaries for protection, rest, and healthy relationships. Take, for instance, God's commandment to observe the Sabbath. Exodus 20:8-11, "Remember the Sabbath day by keeping it holy. Six days you shall labor and do all your work, but the seventh day is a sabbath to the Lord your God. On it you shall not do any work, neither you, nor your son or daughter, nor your male or female servant, nor your animals, nor any foreigner residing in your towns. For in six days the Lord made the heavens and the earth, the sea, and all that is in them, but he rested on the seventh day. Therefore, the Lord blessed the Sabbath day and made it holy." This is essentially a boundary around time, specifically set aside for rest and spiritual renewal. It shows the importance God places on rest and the boundaries necessary to protect it.

Jesus Himself set boundaries. He often withdrew from crowds to pray: Luke 5:16 "Jesus often withdrew to lonely places and prayed."

He also wasn't shy about setting relational boundaries, even with His disciples, when necessary, as we saw in Mark 1:35-37, "Very early in the morning, while it was still dark, Jesus got up, left the house and went off to a solitary place, where he prayed. Simon and his companions went to look for him, and when they found him, they exclaimed: "Everyone is looking for you!"

These examples illustrate that setting boundaries is a practical skill for managing life's demands and a spiritual discipline that enhances our relationship with God and others. Just as Ecclesiastes 3:1 reminds us, "There is a time for everything, and a season for every activity under the heavens." Setting boundaries acknowledges the divine wisdom in recognizing the appropriate times and seasons for different aspects of our lives. By respecting these rhythms, we create space for growth, rest, and deeper connections with God and those around us.

Practical Steps to Establish and Maintain Boundaries

So, how do you go about setting these crucial boundaries? First, identify the areas of your life where boundaries are needed. This might be in your relationships, your work, your use of technology, or even your commitments at church. Reflect on parts of your life that feel overwhelming or draining. Those are areas likely in need of some sturdy fencing.

Next, clearly communicate your boundaries to others. You can be honest and direct about it without being harsh. For example, if you decide not to check work emails after 6 PM so you can spend time with your family or engage in personal rest, communicate this boundary to your colleagues and superiors. Explain the importance of this boundary and how it helps you be more present and productive during work hours.

In line with our discussion on media influence, it's imperative to establish boundaries around your media consumption. This could entail "unfriending" or "unfollowing" individuals whose postings provoke negative emotions or clash with your core beliefs and desired lifestyle. Additionally, consider setting limits on how much news you consume. It's possible to intercede for our world's challenges without immersing yourself in the distressing details of global strife every single day.

Safeguarding your mental space is critical.

Handling Boundary Pushbacks

What happens when your boundaries aren't respected? It's common to face resistance, especially if setting boundaries is new in your relationships or workplace. Some might test the fences. So, you need to be firm and consistent. Politely yet firmly, reiterate your boundaries. Let's say a friend keeps calling during your designated quiet time with God. Remind them of your boundary and suggest an alternative time for a call.

It's also important to manage your feelings of guilt or fear when setting and enforcing boundaries. Remember, setting boundaries is not selfish; it's necessary for your mental health and spiritual well-being. Like any new skill, it takes practice, but each time you successfully maintain a boundary, you strengthen your ability to protect your mental garden, ensuring it remains a place of peace and growth.

5.3 FROM OVERWHELMED TO IN CONTROL: TACTICAL STEPS TO SIMPLIFY YOUR THOUGHT LIFE

Have you ever felt like your mind is a browser with 100 tabs open, each buzzing with reminders, to-dos, and maybe a random video of a cat playing the piano? It's easy to feel overwhelmed when your mental space is cluttered with everything from daily chores to deep-seated worries. But fear not! Let's roll up our sleeves and tackle this mental mess with divine decluttering strategies that can bring you from chaos to clarity.

Identify Sources of Mental Clutter

First, let's pinpoint what's clogging up your mental gears. The biggest culprits are often unfinished tasks, unresolved conflicts, or unrelenting perfectionism. Each of these can create a persistent background noise in your mind, making it hard to focus on the present moment. Start by making a list—yes, the good old-fashioned way with pen and paper—of everything that's on your mind, no matter how big or small. This could range from a looming work deadline to a nagging feeling that you said the wrong thing at dinner last night. Seeing it all on paper can help you recognize what's really eating up your mental bandwidth.

Strategies for Mental Decluttering

Now, with your list in hand, it's time to triage. Some items will need immediate action, others can be scheduled for later, and some—let's be honest—might not need to be on your list at all. Here's where prioritization comes into play. Ask yourself: What's urgent? What aligns with my long-term goals? This might mean deciding to tackle that big project report now because it's due next week, while rescheduling your closet reorganization for next month. Delegation is your friend here. If there are tasks that someone else can handle (like ordering groceries online or delegating a portion of a project to a colleague), pass the baton!

Elimination is equally crucial. This involves letting go of tasks or commitments that don't add value to your life or align with your priorities. It's saying no to organizing the community bake sale because you know it will stretch you too thin. Remember, every 'no' to something non-essential is a 'yes' to something that matters more to you.

Role of Spiritual Disciplines in Gaining Control

In the whirlwind of our daily routines, spiritual disciplines like fasting, solitude, and silence can seem like luxuries we can't afford. But, believe it or not, these practices are not just for monks in a monastery; they're for anyone looking to clear mental clutter and reconnect with God's guidance. Fasting, whether from food, social media, or excessive shopping, helps quiet the noise that distracts us from God's voice. Solitude offers a pause, a chance to breathe and listen to what God is saying without the chorus of daily demands. Silence, especially in our buzz-filled world, can feel awkward initially, but it trains us to be comfortable with being still, making space for God's whispers to reach our hearts.

Integrating these disciplines doesn't have to be daunting. Start small. Choose one day a month to fast from a particular distraction. Spend just ten minutes in solitude each morning, coffee in hand, letting your soul catch up with your body. Gradually, as these practices become part of your routine, you'll notice a shift in how you manage your thoughts and emotions, moving from reactive to reflective, from overwhelmed to in control.

Maintaining a Simplified Thought Life

Keeping your mental space clear is an ongoing process, much like tending a garden. Regular check-ins are key. Set a weekly time to review your priorities and adjust your commitments accordingly. This might mean turning down an invitation to a social event because you know you need a quiet evening to recharge. Embrace flexibility, knowing that what works one month might need tweaking the next.

Also, keep your spiritual discipline in check. Are you maintaining your practice of solitude? Have you found yourself skipping your morning prayer because you hit the snooze button one too many times? Regularly revisiting and renewing your commitments to these practices will help you stay centered and connected to God's peace, no matter what life throws your way.

You can transform your overwhelmed mind into a well-organized hub of peace and productivity by identifying the sources of your mental clutter, employing strategic decluttering, integrating spiritual disciplines, and maintaining regular check-ins. Remember, the goal isn't to achieve a perfectly calm mind at all times—that's pretty much impossible—but to cultivate a mental environment where you can thrive, not just survive. So, take these steps, adjust as you go, and watch your thought life become less of a frantic react-a-thon and more of a purpose-driven peace zone.

5.4 THE HABIT OF GRATITUDE: TRANSFORMING THOUGHTS THROUGH THANKFULNESS

Psychological Benefits of Gratitude

Recall those days filled with mishaps: your alarm fails to sound, the coffee pot malfunctions and your inbox is a minefield. Then, enter gratitude, not merely as a pleasant idea but as a potent mechanism for reshaping your perspective, turning calamities into manageable situations. Research backed by robust scientific evidence—reveals that gratitude profoundly diminishes stress and enhances joy. It's like applying a soothing balm to your frazzled nerves, morphing tension into tranquility.

Gratitude weaves its transformative power by shifting your gaze from the absent or disordered elements in your life to what is present and uplifting. It involves cherishing the small delights and achievements, even amidst challenging periods. This adjustment in focus elevates your mood; it fundamentally changes your brain's wiring.

Engaging in regular gratitude practices boosts the production of serotonin and dopamine, the brain's feel-good neurotransmitters, effectively flipping a switch to brighten your mood. This not only fortifies you against daily pressures but, from a scriptural viewpoint, embodies a form of worship. The Bible is replete with exhortations to give thanks, presenting gratitude not merely as an admirable habit but as a divine command that aligns our spirits with the heart of God by shifting our focus from what's missing or chaotic in our life to what's present and positive. It's about noticing the small joys and victories, even on tough days. This shift isn't just about feeling better; it's about rewiring your brain.

Cultivating a Practice of Gratitude

So, how can you weave gratitude into your daily tapestry so it becomes more than just a Thanksgiving guest? Start simple: keep a gratitude journal. Each night, jot down three things you're thankful for. These don't have to be groundbreaking—sometimes, it's the 'coffee tasted exceptionally good' kind of days that bring the most joy. This practice ends your day on a positive note and helps you pay more attention to the good throughout your day, knowing you'll jot it down later.

Family traditions around thankfulness can also be wonderfully enriching. How about starting a gratitude jar? Have family members write down something they're thankful for each week and drop it in the jar. Then, make a ritual of reading these notes together once a month, turning it into a celebration of all the small blessings that often go unnoticed. This not only cultivates a habit of gratitude but strengthens family bonds.

Gratitude in Difficult Circumstances

Now, expressing gratitude when the skies are blue is one thing, but finding it when they're gray? That's where true resilience is built. It's about looking for a glimmer of light in the darkness. Maybe it's appreciating the support of friends during tough times or the growth that comes from facing your challenges head-on. This isn't about denying the hard stuff; it's about broadening your perspective to see beyond it.

When you practice finding something to be grateful for, even on rainy days, you develop a kind of mental toughness that doesn't just endure but finds a way to grow, no matter the circumstances. It's like training your mental muscles to lift weights—the weights don't get lighter, but you get stronger.

5.5 SERVING OTHERS: HOW GIVING BACK TRANSFORMS OUR THOUGHTS

Biblical Basis for Service

From Genesis to Revelation, the Bible consistently echoes a clear call to serve others. Jesus, in a moment of profound humility and service, washed His disciples' feet, radically redefining the essence of authentic leadership. He didn't merely advocate for service; He embodied it, illustrating that our hands are destined to elevate those around us. Every gesture of kindness, no matter its size, contributes to advancing His kingdom on Earth.

But why does God emphasize service so much? It's simple yet profound—serving others reflects God's own heart. When we serve, we mirror His love and compassion to the world. It's like we're translators, turning divine love into a language people can understand through our actions. Whenever you help someone in need, share a word of encouragement, or volunteer your time, you're broadcasting God's love loud and clear. Think of Matthew 25:40, where Jesus says, "Truly I tell you, whatever you did for one of the least of these brothers and sisters of mine, you did for me." That's God's way of saying, "When you serve them, you're serving Me." It's a direct line between our acts of kindness and God's heart.

Psychological Rewards of Helping Others

This journey of service comes with a fantastic twist: when you serve, it's not just the recipients who get a boost—you do, too! It's like an emotional boomerang; what you send out comes back to you with added joy. It comes back to you in good measure, pressed down, shaken together and running over (Luke 6:38)! Studies have shown that altruism lights up the same parts of the brain that are stimulated by rewards like food or money. Food and money, y'all!

It's the brain saying, "This feels good; let's do it again!" This isn't just feel-good fluff; it's a neurological fact.

Serving others can significantly dial down our stress levels and bathe our brains in feel-good hormones. Ever heard of the "helper's high"? It's a real thing. It's that surge of euphoria you feel when you do something good for someone else. This high is accompanied by a longer-lasting period of improved emotional well-being. In other words, kindness is a natural antidepressant. Plus, focusing on others can help shift our perspective from our problems, giving us a mental break and reducing feelings of anxiety and isolation. It's a win-win of the best kind.

Practical Ways to Serve

The opportunities to serve are as varied as the needs around us. If you're a social butterfly, volunteering at a local shelter or community center might be right up your alley. Love the coziness of home? How about knitting blankets for newborns in hospitals or baking for a neighbor? More of a tech whiz? Offer to help a local non-profit optimize its website or manage its online presence. The key is to match your skills and passions with the needs you see around you.

For those with tight schedules, serving doesn't need to be time-consuming. It could be as simple as offering to pray for someone or sending an encouraging text. Or maybe it's letting someone go ahead of you in line when you're not in a rush. Look for small ways to serve throughout your day. These little acts might seem like drops in the ocean, but remember, the ocean wouldn't be the same without those drops.

Serving changes us, molding us into more compassionate, empathetic, and happier individuals. It renews our minds, refreshes our spirits, and realigns our focus with what truly matters—not just living for ourselves but for others and God. So, why not step out today and find a way to serve? The world needs more kindness, and it starts with you.

5.6 EVENING WIND-DOWN RITUALS: REFLECTIVE PRAYER AND JOURNALING

If you find that morning routines are overwhelming or simply don't align with your natural rhythm, that's perfectly fine. You can turn your evenings into gateways to deeper peace and spiritual insight. They can become your nightly retreat, a sacred time to decompress mentally and connect with God on a profound level. This can set the stage for restful sleep and a refreshed spirit, ready to embrace the challenges of a new day with grace and strength.

Benefits of Evening Rituals

How you end your day can significantly influence how you start the next. Evening rituals help to ease the transition from the busyness of daily life into a more reflective and restful state. This isn't just about getting better sleep; it's about enriching your spiritual life and enhancing your mental health. These rituals can serve as a mental and spiritual "decompression chamber," releasing the pressures of the day and aligning your heart with God's peace. Slowing down and turning inward is invaluable; it allows you to sift through the day's experiences, learn from them, and let go of any lingering stress or anxiety. It's like giving your soul a gentle debrief, ensuring you don't carry today's burdens into tomorrow.

Guided Reflective Prayer

One powerful tool in your evening ritual arsenal is reflective prayer. Evening prayer isn't about rattling off a list of requests to God but rather engaging in a dialogue that reflects on the day's events, your reactions, and God's presence through it all. Start with gratitude; thank God for the day's blessings, seen and unseen. Then, move into a time of confession and reflection—be honest about where you struggled, what emotions you felt, and where you might have fallen short. Ask God for His forgiveness and for the wisdom to handle similar situations better in the future.

Here's a structured guide to help you along:

1. Opening Acknowledgment: Begin by acknowledging God's sovereignty and love. A simple acknowledgment might be, "Lord, You are my peace and my guide, and I trust You with my day (Isaiah 26:3)."
2. Thanksgiving: Reflect on at least three specific moments from the day you are thankful for.
3. Confession and Self-Reflection: Review any moments you wish you had handled differently. Confess these, and ask for God's strength and wisdom.
4. Intercession: Bring before God the needs of others and any ongoing situations in your life.
5. Listening: Conclude with silence, allowing God to speak to your heart.

This prayer format not only guides you through a comprehensive spiritual reflection but also ensures that your focus shifts from the external to the internal, from the hectic to the peaceful.

Spiritual Journaling Practices

Spiritual journaling can deepen your insights and track your spiritual growth over time, complementing your reflective prayer. Journaling about your prayers, insights, struggles, and victories creates a spiritual logbook to reflect on and see how far you've come. It's also a practical way to process emotions and clarify your thoughts.

To get started, keep a dedicated journal for your spiritual reflections. Each evening, after your reflective prayer, jot down key
points, any scriptures that came to mind, and what you feel God
might be saying to you. Use prompts to enrich your journaling,
such as, "Today, I saw God in..." or "A situation I need wisdom for
is...". Over time, your journal will become a treasured roadmap of
your spiritual journey, filled with personal revelations and
reminders of God's faithfulness. Remember to add dates to your
entries.

Creating a Calming Environment

To truly benefit from your evening rituals, create an environment
that encourages relaxation and reflection. This might mean
transforming a corner of your room into a cozy nook with
comfortable pillows, soft lighting, and perhaps some soothing
instrumental music. Minimize distractions by turning off elec-
tronic devices or using them minimally and with purpose, such
as playing soft background music or reading an online
devotional.

If you are into aromatherapy, consider incorporating elements
that engage your senses and enhance your relaxation—aromatic
candles with calming scents like lavender or jasmine or a warm
cup of herbal tea can be perfect accompaniments to your evening
ritual. These small touches create a physically soothing
atmosphere and signal to your mind and body that it's time to
slow down and shift into a reflective mode. We will delve deeper
into sacred spaces after the next couple of sections.

By establishing these evening wind-down rituals, you create not
just a routine but a rhythm of peace that echoes through your
nights and enriches your days. It's about ending each day with
intention, reflection, and peace, setting a sacred tone that nurtures
your sleep and your soul.

5.7 WEEKLY REVIEW: ASSESSING SPIRITUAL GROWTH AND MENTAL HEALTH

Purpose of a Weekly Review

Why should you add another item to your already-packed to-do list? It's about pausing in our fast-paced lives to reflect on our spiritual health and mental well-being, ensuring that our daily practices are truly nurturing our souls. Reviews are not about self-judgment; they are about self-awareness, a kind and curious look at how we're growing in our faith and mental health. It's a checkpoint—a moment to breathe, evaluate, and adjust. It's about taking a proactive stance on your spiritual and mental health rather than just hoping for the best.

Regular inventory helps you catch minor issues before they become big problems, much like spotting weeds when they're tiny sprouts. Are you feeling more anxious lately? Has your prayer life deepened or dwindled? Are you feeling closer to God, or does He seem distant? These aren't always easy questions, but they're crucial. Regular reviews can help you understand where you are on your spiritual path and what adjustments might be needed to align more closely with God's will for your life.

Components of a Weekly Review

First, consider your prayer life. Reflect on both the frequency and depth of your prayers. Are you rushing through them or taking time to really connect with God? Next, review your scripture engagement. How often did you read the Bible this week? What verses stood out, and why? Also, glance through your spiritual journal if you keep one. What themes or concerns have been recurring? This can strongly indicate where God is working in your life or where you're perhaps struggling and need more divine intervention.

Remember to review your adherence to spiritual practices. Maybe you've committed to weekly community service or daily meditation. How consistently have you kept these commitments? What challenges did you face, and what benefits have you noticed? This part of the review helps you see the intentions and impact of your spiritual disciplines, adjusting as needed to stay on track.

Setting Goals for the Coming Week

With insights from your review fresh in your mind, setting goals for the upcoming week can be incredibly effective. These shouldn't be lofty, unreachable goals but small, achievable steps that move you closer to where you want to be spiritually and mentally. Perhaps you've noticed your prayer life waning; you might set a goal to spend ten extra minutes in prayer each morning. Or, if a particular scripture has impacted you, you might want to study that passage more deeply or memorize it.

Setting these goals gives you a clear focus for the week ahead, turning your reflections into action. It's about moving from a reactive spiritual life to a proactive one, where you're not just going through the motions but actively cultivating your relationship with God.

Encouragement for Continuous Growth

Finally, wrap up your weekly review with some encouragement for yourself. Like any growth, spiritual growth isn't a straight line; it's full of ups and downs. Remind yourself of the progress you've already made. Celebrate the victories, no matter how small, and extend grace to yourself for the areas where growth is slower. Encouragement is fuel for perseverance, reminding you that while the road may be challenging, the journey is worth it.

Encouragement can also come from Scripture. Verses like Philippians 1:6, which assures us that "He who began a good work in you will carry it on to completion until the day of Christ Jesus," can be incredibly reassuring. It reminds us that we aren't doing this alone; God is with us, continually working in and through us.

Your weekly review is a spiritual audit, a chance to align your daily living with your highest values and deepest beliefs. Over time, this practice can transform your spiritual life and everyday happiness and resilience. So, take this time each week to pause, reflect, and adjust. Your future self—and your soul—will thank you for it.

5.8 MANAGING TIME WISELY: BIBLICAL PRINCIPLES AND MODERN TECHNIQUES

Do you ever feel like you're trying to stuff a week's worth of activities into a single day? You're not alone. In our fast-paced world, managing time wisely isn't just an excellent skill; it's essential for keeping our sanity intact! But here's the good news: the Bible offers timeless wisdom about managing our days that can be beautifully paired with modern techniques, not just to survive but to thrive.

Biblical Insights on Time Management

Ephesians 5:15-16 admonishes us to "Be very careful, then, how you live—not as unwise but as wise, making the most of every opportunity because the days are evil." This isn't about filling every moment with activity; it's about recognizing the value of our time and using it wisely with a purpose that aligns with God's will. It's a call to prioritize what truly matters and differentiate between what feels urgent and what is genuinely important. This scripture reminds us that our time is a gift from God, and how we use it reflects our stewardship of that gift.

In a world that constantly demands our attention and energy, this passage encourages us to be intentional with our choices. It challenges us to discern and focus on what advances our spiritual growth and fulfills God's purposes in our lives. By setting boundaries and making deliberate decisions, we can create space for meaningful relationships, personal renewal, and service to others, all of which honor God. This wise use of time ultimately leads to a more balanced, fulfilling life that bears witness to God's goodness and grace.

Practical Time Management Strategies

Now, how do we marry this biblical wisdom with practical, everyday strategies? One effective modern technique is time blocking. Imagine your day as a series of blocks, each dedicated to a specific task. This method helps you allocate time and minimizes distractions, allowing you to focus entirely on the task at hand. For instance, you might block an hour each morning for devotion and prayer, ensuring your spiritual nourishment before the day's demands kick in.

Another strategy is prioritization, guided by the Pareto Principle, often known as the 80/20 rule: 80% of results come from 20% of efforts. Identify the tasks that have the most significant impact on your spiritual life, relationships, and responsibilities. Focus on these, and you'll find your efforts are more productive and less scattered.

Integrating Time Management with Spiritual Goals

Integrating these strategies with your spiritual goals can be a game-changer. For example, if one of your spiritual goals is to read through the Bible in a year, you could set a specific time block each day for reading a chapter or two. This commitment turns into a scheduled appointment with God, one you're more likely to keep because it's on your calendar, and so woven into the fabric of your day.

Similarly, if you aim to grow in prayer, you might prioritize a weekly hour-long slot to visit a local park or quiet space where you can talk to God without interruptions. By scheduling these practices, you make them as critical as any meeting or appointment, which honors God and deepens your spiritual journey.

Tools and Resources

Thankfully, we have numerous tools in this digital age that can help us manage our time effectively. Apps like Google Calendar or Microsoft Outlook can be fantastic for time blocking, allowing you to set reminders for your daily prayer time or weekly Bible study. For those who prefer something less digital, a good old-fashioned planner can work wonders. You can even find planners designed specifically for Christians, which include daily scripture verses and spaces to write down prayer requests and blessings, integrating time management with spiritual reflection.

Tools like Trello or Asana can help you prioritize your tasks, clarifying what you need to focus on each day. These can be especially helpful in managing church projects or community service efforts, ensuring that you're making the most of your time and energy in serving others.

In essence, managing your time wisely is more than just keeping a schedule; it's about ensuring that your daily activities reflect your deepest values and spiritual commitments. It's about making time for God in the whirlwind of life and using each day He gives us to the fullest. With biblical principles as your foundation and modern techniques as your tools, you can transform your time management from a source of stress to a channel of blessing for yourself and those you serve. So, take a moment today to ask yourself: how can I use my time to reflect God's purpose in my life? The answer could reshape your days, turning every moment into an opportunity for growth and grace.

5.9 CREATING A SANCTUARY AT HOME: SACRED SPACES FOR PEACE AND PRAYER

Imagine transforming a corner of your home or garden into a little slice of heaven—a peaceful nook where the hustle of the world fades away, and you become enveloped in calm and serenity. This space becomes your spiritual sanctuary, a dedicated place for prayer, meditation, and quiet reflection, enhancing your connection with God. It's like setting up a private chapel within your four walls, where you can retreat to recharge your spiritual batteries and find peace amidst life's chaos.

Importance of a Dedicated Spiritual Space

Why carve out a dedicated space for spiritual practices at home? Well, just as you have specific areas for eating, sleeping, and relaxing, having a designated spiritual space helps to cultivate a routine and mindset that prioritizes your relationship with God. It's about creating a physical reminder and a set location that beckons you to come, sit, pray, and meditate. This space serves as a tangible expression of your commitment to your spiritual journey, making it easier to transition from the busyness of your daily life into a state of spiritual contemplation and intimacy with God.

Designing Your Sanctuary

Creating your personal sanctuary doesn't require a complete home makeover. Start by choosing a spot that feels right to you. It could be a quiet corner of your bedroom, a spare room, or even a section of your living room. The key is consistency and association; over time, just entering this space will naturally cue your mind and body to enter a state of peace and readiness for spiritual activities.

When designing your sanctuary, incorporate elements that inspire and uplift your spirit. Start with a comfortable seat—perhaps a cushioned chair or a plush pillow on the floor. Add a small table or shelf for your Bible, a notebook, and maybe some inspirational reading material. Decorate the space with items that speak to your faith and enhance your focus—crosses, icons, or even a small vase of fresh flowers can be beautiful reminders of God's creation. Consider including a candle to light during your prayer time, symbolizing the light of Christ and the presence of the Holy Spirit.

Personalize your space with scriptures that resonate deeply with you. These can be beautifully framed or even artistically written on paper or canvas. Choose verses that encourage, challenge, and comfort you. Surrounding yourself with God's Word visually not only beautifies the space but also steers your thoughts towards Him during your time there.

Using Your Sanctuary

Establish a routine that fits into your daily life. Morning is ideal for starting your day centered and calm, or evenings may work better to wrap up your day with reflection and gratitude. Use this space for various spiritual activities: engage in scripture reading, where you quietly read and meditate on God's Word; dedicate time for prayer, both speaking to God and listening; practice spiritual journaling, recording insights, prayers, and reflections; or simply sit in silence, allowing yourself to bask in God's presence.

This space is also perfect for family devotions. Invite your family members to join you in prayer or scripture reading, strengthening your collective faith and providing a model of spiritual discipline. For meditation, guide your family through simple, focused meditations on a scripture or a spiritual theme, teaching them to quiet their minds and listen to God.

Maintaining a Sacred Atmosphere

Keeping your spiritual sanctuary sacred involves regular upkeep, both physically and spiritually. Keep the area clean and tidy, treating it with the same respect you would a church or place of worship. This respect underscores the significance of the space and your activities there.

It's also essential to maintain the area's tranquility. Decide that this space is for peace and prayer, not for work or other stressful activities. This distinction helps preserve the sanctuary atmosphere and ensures that when you enter the space, your mind and heart prepare for communion with God.

Creating and using a dedicated spiritual space in your home provides a tangible way to meet with God daily. This sanctuary becomes a vital part of your spiritual discipline, a physical manifestation of your faith, and a continual reminder of God's peace and presence. It's a small piece of heaven in your home, a sacred corner where you meet with God, grow in your faith, and find peace amid the storms of life.

As we conclude this chapter, remember that each small practice, each quiet moment spent in your home sanctuary, builds your spiritual resilience and deepens your relationship with God. These daily practices are not just routines; they are the threads that weave a vibrant tapestry of faith that can hold firm against life's challenges. With your home sanctuary as a cornerstone of your spiritual practice, you're equipped to face each day with peace and purpose. As we move forward, let's carry this tranquility and focus into every aspect of our lives, allowing our everyday actions to reflect our deep-rooted faith.

CHAPTER 6 UNMASKING THE UMBRELLA LIES

"Do not conform to the pattern of this world, but be transformed by the renewing of your mind. Then you will be able to test and approve what God's will is—his good, pleasing and perfect will."

— *ROMANS* 12:2

The pursuit of perfection can be likened to chasing a mirage. Just when it seems within reach, it evaporates, leaving you grasping at the air. In a culture saturated with idealized portrayals and the facade of flawless existence on social media, the drive toward perfection often becomes an automatic response. Yet, this endeavor is as fruitless as attempting to capture the wind in your grasp. Let's explore the truth behind this myth of perfection.

Exposing the Cultural Origins and Perpetuation of Perfectionism

First, let's talk about where this obsession with perfection comes from. It's like a well-meaning gift from a society that's actually a Trojan horse. Media, social influences, and yes, sometimes even our church cultures have painted a picture of what the 'ideal' woman should look like: a perfect home, perfect body, perfect kids, and perfect faith.

Magazines scream at us from the shelves with headlines that promise to reveal the secrets to becoming flawless, and social media feeds are littered with curated glimpses of perfect lives. Even in some church circles, there can be an unspoken pressure to present a polished version of ourselves, masking our struggles and doubts with a veneer of 'I've got it all together.'

This cultural script reads like a manual for setting up unrealistic standards that are more about appearances than genuine self-improvement. It's a recipe for discouragement because, let's face it, who can live up to these Photoshopped realities?

The Psychological Impact of Striving for Perfection

Now, let's dive into the deep end—how chasing this illusion impacts your mental health. Striving for perfection is like setting up camp on a treadmill; you keep running but never get anywhere. This relentless pursuit can lead to a buffet of mental health challenges, including anxiety, depression, and burnout. Why? Because constantly falling short of unattainable standards is exhausting and disheartening. It's like being in a race where the finish line keeps moving further away.

Anxiety often bubbles up when you feel like you're not measuring up, and depression can sneak in when you feel defeated by the constant pressure to perform. And burnout? It's the natural outcome of pushing yourself too hard for too long, trying to be all things to all people all the time.

Biblical Examples of Grace and Imperfection

But here's the Good News—God isn't looking for perfection. He's looking for progress, for hearts that turn to Him in their imperfection. The Bible is brimming with stories of people who were anything but perfect. Take David, for instance, a man after God's own heart, who was also an adulterer and a murderer. Despite his grievous sins, David's story is one of repentance, forgiveness, and a renewed commitment to God. His life shows us that no failure is too great for God's redeeming love and that a contrite heart can restore our relationship with Him.

Similarly, consider Peter, who denied Christ three times during His arrest and trial. Peter's denial was a moment of profound weakness and fear, yet it did not disqualify him from being a key figure in the early church. After Jesus' resurrection, Peter was restored and empowered to become a leading apostle, boldly proclaiming the gospel. This transformation highlights that our past mistakes do not define our future in God's plan. God's grace is sufficient to turn our shortcomings into strengths and our failures into testimonies of His mercy and power.

These stories are not in the Scriptures to give us a scandalous edge; they remind us that God uses imperfect people to carry out His perfect plans. They encourage us to embrace our imperfections and seek God's guidance and strength. Instead of striving for unattainable perfection, we are called to grow in faith, to rely on God's grace, and to trust that He can work through our weaknesses. This perspective brings hope and fosters a deeper relationship with God as we learn to depend on Him more fully and witness His transformative work in our lives.

These Biblical heroes were not celebrated for their perfection but for their reliance on God's grace. Their lives remind us that perfection is not the goal; faithfulness is.

Practical Steps to Embrace Imperfection

So, how do we break free from this perfection trap? Start by setting realistic goals. Life is not a Pinterest board; it's messy, beautiful, and wonderfully imperfect. Set goals that challenge you but are achievable. Celebrate small victories and understand that every step forward is progress.

Next, practice self-compassion. Speak to yourself like you would to a dear friend. When you stumble, instead of criticizing yourself, offer words of encouragement. Remember, God's grace is sufficient for you, and His power is made perfect in your weakness (2 Corinthians 12:9).

Lastly, reframe failures as opportunities for growth. Each mistake is a masterclass in disguise, teaching you something valuable. Consider Thomas Edison, who famously said about his journey to invent the light bulb, "I have not failed. I've just found 10,000 ways that won't work." So, instead of beating yourself up, ask, "What can I learn from this?" This shift in perspective can transform your approach to mistakes and setbacks, turning them into stepping stones rather than stumbling blocks.

By unmasking this lie of perfection, you can begin to appreciate the beauty of your real, raw, and remarkable journey. Let go of the illusion, embrace your imperfections, and walk in the freedom of God's all-sufficient grace. Remember, it's not about being perfect; it's about being perfected in Him.

6.2 OVERCOMING THE "NOT ENOUGH" SYNDROME: SCRIPTURAL AFFIRMATIONS FOR SELF-WORTH

"You're not smart enough," "You're not good enough," or "You don't belong here." Do any of these insidious doubts ring a bell? Doubts about self-worth can infiltrate the most private spaces of your life, the bustle of your professional environment, and even the hallowed halls of your place of worship, instilling a pervasive sense of inadequacy as if you're constantly lagging.

Intrinsic Worth Over Perfection

Think about the last time you felt you weren't measuring up. Was it when scrolling through social media, seeing snapshots of others' curated perfection? Or perhaps during a meeting at work where you couldn't find the courage to voice your thoughts, plagued by the feeling that your ideas weren't sharp enough? Maybe it's during those moments when your spiritual life feels stagnant, and you believe you're not devout enough compared to others who seem to live their faith so effortlessly. These scenarios are just a few stages where the "not enough" syndrome can play out, casting a shadow over your self-esteem and worth.

The reality is the Bible never places value on perfection or societal metrics of success. Instead, it emphasizes intrinsic worth derived from being created in God's image. Consider Matthew 10:29-31, where Jesus speaks about sparrows sold for a penny, yet not one falls to the ground outside the Father's care. He then reassures us, "So don't be afraid; you are worth more than many sparrows." This passage highlights God's intimate care and value for each of us, underscoring that our worth is not based on external achievements but on God's unwavering love and attention.

Additionally, Ephesians 2:10 tells us, "For we are God's handiwork, created in Christ Jesus to do good works, which God prepared in advance for us to do." This scripture reinforces the idea that our value is inherent and rooted in our creation by God. We are crafted with purpose and intention, designed to fulfill good works that God has already set out for us. Our worth is not contingent on meeting societal standards or achieving certain milestones but is grounded in our identity as God's unique and purposeful creations.

These scriptures are not just words but the foundation of your identity, affirming that you are enough because you are His. When we internalize this truth, we can let go of the relentless pursuit of perfection and societal validation. Instead, we can rest in the knowledge that our value is fixed and immutable, rooted in God's love and purpose for our lives. This shift in perspective allows us to live more authentically and confidently, embracing our God-given identity and the unique path He has set before us.

6.3 THE MYTH OF 'SUPPOSED TO': RESHAPING EXPECTATIONS WITH BIBLICAL INSIGHTS

Imagine your life as a journey unfolding before you, where each unexpected turn triggers an internal "Recalculating!" alert. Feeling disconnected from the grand orchestra of life becomes all too common when we're inundated by the "shoulds" from society, family, and our inner critics. This chapter encourages you to lower the volume of these external pressures and attune yourself to the unique melody God has composed specifically for you—a melody that might resemble jazz's spontaneous flow more than classical music's structured notes.

Challenge Societal and Personal Expectations

Expectations often masquerade as the standard, the societal benchmark of what's considered 'normal.' Yet, what is normality but a construct? Society parades a sequence of life milestones - attaining a degree by 22, walking down the aisle by 30, acquiring a home by 35 - that dictates a rhythm many find hard to match. Family expectations can also play a symphony of their own, with relatives inadvertently imposing their own life scripts for us to follow, note for note. Just as formidable are the standards we impose upon ourselves, serving as rigorous conductors in our quest for a perfection that frequently eludes our grasp.

Living under the weight of these "supposed tos" can cramp your style, leaving you feeling confined and out of sync with your true self. Life isn't a one-size-fits-all melody. It's a dynamic, evolving composition meant to be as unique as each person performing it.

Biblical Example of God's Unconventional Paths

If you're looking for role models who broke the mold, the Bible's got a whole lineup. Consider David, again; before becoming a king, he was just a shepherd boy—not exactly the resume you'd expect for a future monarch. His path was anything but conventional, filled with battles, running from Saul, and living in caves, yet he was exactly where God wanted him to be, learning lessons that would later define his reign. David's journey from a humble shepherd to a revered king exemplifies how God can use unexpected circumstances to prepare us for our destinies.

Then there's Mary, a young, unwed woman who found herself pregnant in a culture that could have stoned her for less. Talk about not meeting societal expectations! Yet, despite its staggering deviation from societal norms, her willingness to embrace God's plan led to her role as the mother of Christ. Mary's story is a powerful reminder that God's purposes often transcend societal expectations, and her courage and obedience brought about the most significant event in human history.

And let's not forget Moses. Born into a time when his people were enslaved, Moses' life began with an act of defiance as his mother hid him in a basket to save him from Pharaoh's decree to kill all Hebrew baby boys. Raised in Pharaoh's palace yet profoundly connected to his Hebrew roots, Moses eventually fled to the desert after killing an Egyptian. There, he spent 40 years as a shepherd before God called him from a burning bush to lead the Israelites out of slavery. Moses' journey was marked by self-doubt, exile, and the daunting task of confronting the most powerful ruler of his time. Despite his flaws and fears, Moses became the leader who delivered God's people from bondage, demonstrating that God's call often comes when we least expect it and through people who feel least prepared.

God's plans often defy human expectations, weaving through paths we might never consider. Whether it's a shepherd boy, a young virgin, or a fugitive shepherd, God uses unlikely candidates to fulfill His extraordinary purposes. Each of these individuals embraced God's plan for their lives despite the unconventional paths they had to walk, teaching us that true faith often requires stepping out of our comfort zones and trusting in God's greater vision.

Stay Flexible and Open to God's Plans

Embracing God's unique script for your life requires flexibility—a willingness to stretch and bend with the twists and turns of His plot. This might mean stepping out in faith when opportunities don't fit your meticulously crafted plans or saying no to good options that don't align with God's best.

Staying open to God's leading involves daily surrender and acknowledging that His ways are higher than ours. Isaiah 55:9 reminds us, "Just as the heavens are higher than the earth, My thoughts and My ways are higher than yours." It's about holding your plans with open hands, giving God the space to write His epic narrative through your life. This openness to divine orchestration brings peace and aligns you with the adventures God has in store.

Journaling or Reflection Exercises for Clarity

One practical way to cultivate this openness is through journaling. Why not start a 'Possibilities Journal'? Here, you can jot down all the unexpected, out-of-the-box ways God might be leading you. Whenever you encounter a Bible story or a real-life story that resonates with your journey, add it to your journal. Reflect on these entries regularly, and you'll likely start to see a pattern of God's unexpected moves in your life and the lives of others.

This practice can help crystallize your thoughts and prayers, giving you a clearer vision of where God might be directing your next steps. It's about turning your 'supposed to' into 'could be,' allowing God's creative direction to lead you into richer and more fulfilling narratives than you could have scripted on your own.

By reshaping your expectations with biblical insights and embracing the unique melody God has composed for you, you can live out a story that's not only fulfilling but also gloriously divine. So, close the conventional playbook and let your life be a testament to God's limitless imagination and perfect timing.

6.4 "I CAN'T CHANGE": DEBUNKING THE LIE WITH NEUROPLASTICITY AND SCRIPTURE

Are you sometimes concerned that your mind is set in its ways, ensnared by the same habits and thought patterns you've lived with for years? Picture yourself moving through a dance that was choreographed in the distant past, dancing to a tune that no longer plays. This experience might be described as succumbing to the belief that "you can't teach an old dog new tricks." However, the truth is quite the opposite: your mind is not rigid like concrete but is flexible and malleable, much like clay, thanks to the wonders of neuroplasticity.

Neuroplasticity in Simple Terms

Neuroplasticity might sound like a term from a sci-fi movie or even plastic surgery for your brain. However, it's actually your brain's incredible ability to reorganize itself by forming new neural connections throughout life. Imagine your brain as a garden. Initially, the paths in this garden—your neural pathways— are determined by your regular thoughts and behaviors. But every time you learn something new or change a habit, you create new pathways. It's like forging new trails in your garden. This means that no matter your age or stage in life, your brain is capable of change, capable of growth, and capable of transformation.

This ability to adapt and evolve is not just fascinating; it's empowering. It means the things you once believed were unchangeable— like persistent negative thoughts, deep-seated fears, or ingrained behaviors—are actually not set in stone. You can reroute those paths. You can grow new flowers. The "I can't change" narrative? That's just an old excuse and an old tune. It's time to change the music.

Neuroplasticity Linked to Biblical Renewal

Romans 12:2 doesn't just suggest but commands us not to conform to the pattern of this world but to be transformed by the renewing of our minds. The Contemporary English Version of the bible says, "Don't be like the people of this world but let God change the way you think. Then you will know how to do everything that is good and pleasing to him." This isn't just poetic; it's practical. This scripture aligns beautifully with the concept of neuroplasticity. Renewing your mind means more than just adopting a new way of thinking; it's about allowing God to rewire your brain to form new, healthy, God-honoring neural pathways.

This divine call for renewal is not about achieving a one-time change but fostering an ongoing evolution of our minds. It's about choosing to focus daily on thoughts that align with God's truth, thereby physically changing our brain's wiring to default to His perspectives over the world's lies. Each scripture you meditate on, prayer you whisper, and choice to focus on the good is not just spiritual growth but neurological change!

Dispelling Myths About Fixed Traits

Let's tackle another myth: the belief that your traits and habits are fixed. The world might tell you you're just 'set in your ways,' but science and scripture offer a rebuttal. Modern psychology supports the idea that we can change even our most entrenched habits with intentional effort. Biblically, we see time and again that transformation is at the heart of the Christian experience.

Rahab: From Prostitute to Key Figure in Biblical History

Rahab was initially known as a prostitute in the city of Jericho. Despite her past, she displayed remarkable faith by hiding the Israelite spies and acknowledging the power of the God of Israel. Her courageous actions and belief in God led to her and her family's salvation when Jericho fell. This pivotal moment marked the beginning of her transformation from a woman with a tarnished reputation to a key figure in biblical history.

Rahab's story didn't end with Jericho's fall. She went on to become the great-great-grandmother of King David and is listed in the genealogy of Jesus Christ (Matthew 1:5). This transformation illustrates that God can change anyone, regardless of their past, to fulfill a significant role in His plan. Rahab's faith and transformation testify to God's power to redeem and repurpose our lives for His glory.

Mary Magdalene: From Troubled Past to Faithful Disciple

Mary Magdalene is often remembered as a woman from whom Jesus cast out seven demons (Luke 8:2). After her deliverance, she became a devoted follower of Jesus, showing deep love and unwavering support for His ministry. Her transformation from a troubled past to a faithful disciple highlights the profound impact of Jesus' healing power.

Mary Magdalene's devotion was further demonstrated when she became the first to witness the risen Christ. Jesus entrusted her with the crucial task of announcing His resurrection to the disciples (John 20:11-18). Her journey from a life of torment to becoming a pivotal messenger of the resurrection underscores God's ability to redefine our identities and purposes. Mary's story is a powerful example of how God's transformative power can change our lives and equip us for His divine mission.

These stories and the science of neuroplasticity teach us that change is not only possible, it's part of our design. God didn't create us to be static creatures but beings who grow and evolve, who can overcome the past and step into new identities in Christ.

Practical Exercises for Brain Rewiring

So, how do we practically engage in this rewiring? First, focused meditation on scripture is a powerful tool. Choose a verse that speaks to the change you seek, and spend time quietly meditating on it daily. Let the words sink in, rewiring old thoughts of fear, inadequacy, or doubt with truths of strength, sufficiency, and faith.

Memorizing Bible verses is another transformative practice. It's not just about storing words in your memory but embedding divine truth in your brain's wiring. These scriptures become the default pathways your thoughts travel when faced with life's challenges.

Lastly, stepping into new, challenging activities that align with biblical growth can stimulate neuroplasticity. Whether it's joining a ministry, serving in a new capacity, or simply engaging in a new study group, each new activity helps forge new neural pathways, making room for growth and change.

By embracing these practices, you are not just subject to change; you are an active participant in it, working hand in hand with God's transformative power to become not just who you were supposed to be but who you can be. So, let's step off the old tracks and blaze new trails, rewriting our minds with the Word of God and reshaping our brains with the renewing power of His truth.

6.5 THE POWER OF 'YET': TRANSFORMING FAILURES INTO STEPPING STONES

Imagine you're painting a masterpiece, and halfway through, the paint spills, creating a smear across your canvas. You could toss it out, call it ruined, or incorporate that smear into a new, unexpected element of your artwork. This scenario mirrors life's approach to mistakes and failures. If we view them through the lens of a 'growth mindset,' as defined by psychologist Carol Dweck, every spill has the potential to enhance, rather than tarnish, the final picture. A growth mindset embraces challenges, perseveres through setbacks, and views effort as a path to mastery, contrasting sharply with a 'fixed mindset' that dodges challenges and views failures as a reflection of unchangeable abilities.

In the spiritual walk, embracing a growth mindset means recognizing that God is continuously at work within us, refining and reshaping our imperfections for His glory. Let's look at Peter again, one of Jesus' closest disciples, who infamously denied Christ three times. Peter could have succumbed to his failure at that moment, letting it define and end his story. Instead, he experienced profound growth from his mistake, which prepared him to lead the early church with humility and strength. Peter's story didn't end with his failure; it started a new chapter of deeper faith and understanding. His life illustrates that failures aren't final; they're often the first step toward significant spiritual breakthroughs.

How can we apply this mindset to our everyday challenges and setbacks? Start by tweaking your internal dialogue. It's about shifting from "I can't do this" to "I can't do this yet." This small addition of 'yet' is a powerful reminder that your limitations are temporary barriers to your growth journey. For instance, if public speaking at church terrifies you, instead of thinking, "I'm not good at speaking," try, "I'm not good at speaking yet." This perspective opens the door to growth, learning, and the possibility that God will use your developing skills in ways you might not imagine.

To practically foster this mindset, setting small, achievable goals is crucial. These goals act like stepping stones across the river of challenges—they need to be solid enough to support you but spaced closely enough to keep the other side in sight. For example, if you're working on becoming more patient, set a goal to pause and pray for ten seconds before responding in situations that typically trigger a quick, sharp reply. These brief moments of prayerful reflection might seem small, but they can significantly shift how you react under pressure, gradually transforming your responses and enhancing your relationships.

By cultivating this growth mindset, supported by scriptural truths and practical strategies, you can start to see your failures and limitations not as insurmountable walls but as hurdles meant to be cleared, each propelling you closer to who you are in Christ. So, next time you face a setback, remember the power of 'yet'—it's the bridge between 'can't' and 'will,' and it's where God often does His best work, turning our mess into His masterpiece.

As we wrap up this chapter, remember that each failure is not a stop sign but a guideline for growth. The teachings of the Bible reassure us that our shortcomings are fertile ground for spiritual and personal development. Embrace each challenge with a mindset of 'yet,' and watch as your paths bend towards His plans and purposes, transforming every 'cannot' into an opportunity to learn, grow, and eventually triumph.

CHAPTER 7 ADDRESSING SPECIFIC LIFE CHALLENGES WITH SCRIPTURAL GUIDANCE

"I press on toward the goal to win the prize for which God has called me heavenward in Christ Jesus."

— *PHILIPPIANS 3:14*

Navigating life's journey can resemble an intricate balancing dance—equivalent to riding a unicycle and juggling simultaneously. It's an exhilarating experience yet fraught with moments of doubt and trepidation. As women, we face societal expectations to seamlessly juggle numerous roles—whether pursuing a career, seeking spiritual growth, or being the bedrock of our families—all while moving forward with grace and confidence. But what happens when keeping everything in harmony becomes overwhelming? This chapter will act as your guide, steering you through the process of finding equilibrium amid life's challenges and equipping you with the strength to walk life's tightrope with steadfast faith and poise.

7.1 BALANCING WORK AND FAITH: STRATEGIES FOR WORKING WOMEN

Striking a balance between professional responsibilities and spiritual commitments can sometimes seem as challenging as blending oil with water – an endeavor that appears futile. However, the notion that career success and spiritual growth are mutually exclusive is a myth we're ready to debunk. This chapter is dedicated to you, the Christian working woman, offering guidance on how to gracefully weave your faith throughout your workday, thus maintaining a steady pace in both your career and spiritual journey.

Scriptural Encouragement for Working Women

Proverbs 31 vividly paints a portrait of a woman adept at managing both her domestic and professional spheres. Verse 16 shows her thoughtfully assessing a field before buying it, showcasing her wisdom and shrewdness as an investor and entrepreneur. Her dedication shines as she toils into the night, her lamp burning bright, symbolizing her relentless drive and effort. Similarly, Titus 2:7-8 urges us to approach all our tasks with integrity and dedication. Together, these scriptures reinforce the idea that a woman can excel in her career without neglecting her spiritual development. Instead of viewing professional success and spiritual growth as conflicting goals, the Bible presents them as complementary parts of a woman's life, each enhancing the other in meaningful ways.

Practical Work-Faith Balance Techniques

So, how do you keep your spiritual fervor burning amidst the demands of deadlines and meetings? It's all about weaving small, sacred practices into the fabric of your workday. Consider initiating lunchtime prayer walks. These are great for physical health and offer a precious slice of solitude for prayer or listening to a

Bible app. The rhythmic steps and fresh air can be surprisingly conducive to spiritual clarity and calm.

Or, how about marking the start of your workday with a short devotional? Before the emails start flooding in, take a moment to meditate on a Bible verse or a daily devotional piece. This sets a spiritually reflective tone for the day, equipping you with divine wisdom and peace as you tackle your tasks. Think of it as putting on your spiritual armor before stepping onto the battlefield of corporate challenges.

Success Stories

Need a little inspiration? Let's take a leaf from the books of some incredible women who've mastered this balance. Like Sarah, a marketing executive who integrates her faith into her work by starting each team meeting with a moment of reflective silence, allowing everyone to pause and refocus. Or Emily, who has negotiated with her employer to start later so she can attend morning prayer services. Their stories aren't just testimonials; they're proof that with creativity and conviction, you can honor your faith in your work environment.

7.2 SINGLE AND SATISFIED: FINDING CONTENTMENT IN GOD'S PLAN

In the whirlwind of couples' selfies and wedding hashtags, being single can sometimes feel like sitting on the sidelines of a dance floor. But what if I told you that this season could be less about sitting out and more about diving deep into a solo dance of self-discovery and spiritual growth? Paul in 1 Corinthians 7:7-8 throws us a curveball that might just change the game. He suggests that singleness is a special gift, an opportunity not for moping but for significant spiritual and personal development. Imagine that—

singleness, a gift! This isn't just about waiting for the right person but about becoming the right person, fully aligned with God's purpose.

Biblical Perspectives on Singleness

So, let's unpack this gift, shall we? Singleness isn't a pit stop on the way to marriage; it's a unique path to achieving God's plan for your life. This season is ripe with opportunities for growth that are not just about building a better you but about deepening your relationship with your Creator. It's a time when you can make huge strides in your faith, unencumbered by the compromises and complexities that come with partnership and raising children. The Bible highlights this in 1 Corinthians 7:32-35, where Paul talks about the undivided attention to the Lord that singleness affords. Ask the married women! It's about leveraging this less distracted time to serve God wholeheartedly, whether it's through missions, ministry, or personal spiritual disciplines. Think of it as a divine runway, giving you the momentum to take off into a deeper faith journey.

Cultivating Personal Fulfillment

Focusing on personal development doesn't mean you're putting life on hold. It's about enriching it. Engage in activities that light up your spirit and expand your horizons. Take that mission trip you've always dreamed of, enroll in a Bible study that challenges you, or start a ministry that tugs at your heart. These aren't just fillers until 'the one' comes along; they are steps toward fulfilling your divine purpose. And remember, personal fulfillment also comes from community. Dive into your church family, find strength in friendships, and forge bonds that will support you, single or not. These relationships are instrumental in shaping you and reminding you that your value isn't tied to your marital status but to your identity in Christ.

Overcoming Societal Pressure

Of course, it's not all smooth sailing. Society often has ideas about where you should be in life, especially regarding marriage clocks and relationship statuses. But here's where you can stand firm in your faith and the truth of your worth in God. When Aunt Sheila asks about your love life at the family reunion, arm yourself with grace and humor. More importantly, arm yourself with the truth that God's timing is perfect, and His plans are worth the wait. Use scriptures like Psalm 139:16, which reassures us that all our days are written in God's book before one of them came to be. This scripture isn't just a comfort; it's a declaration of God's meticulous care in plotting our life course, single years included. My most profound spiritual growth occurred during eight years of full-time ministry at a local church in South Africa while I was still single. These were glorious years of undistracted devotion to the Lord, even as I navigated the "still single" questions and comments from the "Aunt Sheilas."

Many churches and Christian communities recognize the value of single members and create spaces for growth and fellowship that cater to their unique needs and contributions. You may be called to overseas missions, a calling you may not be able to pursue once you are married.

In embracing singleness, you're not marking time; you're making the most of a precious opportunity. It's a season to invest profoundly in your relationship with God, to serve with undivided attention, and to grow into the person He has called you to be. So, take heart, dive deep into this season, and watch God use your singleness in ways beyond what you could imagine. Your single years can be some of your life's richest, most fruitful seasons if you embrace them with faith, purpose, and a dash of adventure.

7.3 MARRIAGE AND MENTAL HEALTH: NAVIGATING CHALLENGES TOGETHER

Envision your marriage as a shared garden that you and your partner diligently cultivate together. This garden brims with potential, promising beauty and harmony, yet demands ongoing attention and care. Within this collaborative space, each gesture and word can act as life-giving sunlight or nurturing rain, fostering growth. Conversely, neglect can permit weeds to flourish and disorder to prevail. Just as a garden requires consistent watering, weeding, and nurturing a marriage needs continuous effort, intentional acts of love, and thoughtful communication to thrive. Addressing mental health challenges together can strengthen the marital bond, fostering an environment of empathy, support, and resilience.

Navigating mental health challenges in marriage requires a concerted effort to maintain open communication and mutual understanding. Creating a safe space where both partners feel comfortable sharing their struggles without fear of judgment is essential. By prioritizing each other's mental health, couples can work together to identify stressors and develop strategies to cope with them. This might include seeking professional help, engaging in regular physical activity, or practicing relaxation techniques. By actively supporting each other's mental well-being, couples can prevent the "weeds" of resentment, frustration, and misunderstanding from taking root.

Scripture offers enduring guidance for fostering marital unity, emphasizing the importance of mutual respect, love, and support. Ephesians 5:21-33, for example, goes beyond mere advice, compelling couples to mutually submit to one another in reverence for Christ. This reciprocal exchange of support and understanding is the cornerstone of a robust marital foundation. By following these principles, couples can navigate the complexities of mental health together, ensuring that their relationship not only endures but also flourishes. The act of mutually submitting to one another, as Christ modeled, involves bearing each other's burdens and celebrating each other's victories, creating a resilient and nurturing marital garden where both partners can thrive.

Scriptures for a Healthy Marriage

Biblical scriptures like Ephesians 5:21-33 provide a rich and profound blueprint for understanding the sanctity of marriage as a mirror of the profound relationship between Christ and the Church—marked by deep intimacy, selfless sacrifice, and steadfast and unwavering love. These verses illuminate the truth that love transcends mere emotion; it is an active commitment, manifesting in daily acts of kindness, empathetic understanding, and relentless forgiveness. Start each day with a sincere prayer, asking to view your spouse with the same compassion Christ shows us. This shift in perspective is vital for fulfilling your marriage vows with deliberate care and grace.

Communication Skills Grounded in Faith

Effective communication in marriage transforms potential conflicts into harmonious dialogues, much like orchestrating a symphony rather than competing in solitary performances. It's about ensuring that your words build up rather than tear down. James 1:19 advises quick listening, slow speaking, and slow anger. This might mean taking a deep breath before responding to your spouse, ensuring you fully understand their perspective before offering your own. Thinking before you speak can prevent misunderstandings that lead to resentment and distance.

Additionally, grounding your communication in prayer can transform your interactions, making them more about partnership and support than about winning an argument. Together, you can set a time each week to discuss more profound issues, ensuring both can express themselves freely in a spirit of love and mutual respect.

Prayer and Worship as a Couple

Spiritual intimacy can be the glue that holds a marriage together through life's storms. Engaging in joint spiritual practices such as prayer and worship can significantly deepen your connection, aligning you both with God's purpose for your marriage. Prayer together each morning or sharing what you learned from your Bible reading can strengthen your spiritual bond. These moments of shared vulnerability and worship create a strong foundation of faith, which can carry you through times of personal and relational trials. It's about turning towards God together, seeking His guidance, and thanking Him for His blessings, which can infuse your relationship with grace and resilience.

Handling Marital Stress

Let's face it, stress is as much a part of life as breathing, and it can strain even the strongest marriages. However, incorporating scriptural wisdom and psychological insights can equip you to manage these stresses effectively. Philippians 4:6-7 encourages us not to be anxious, but in everything, by prayer and petition, with thanksgiving, present your requests to God. In your marriage, this can mean tackling financial worries, work pressures, or parenting challenges as a team, approaching each issue with prayer and proactive planning. When stress arises, remind each other of God's promises to provide peace that transcends understanding, and make a plan to tackle the stressors together, whether it's through setting a budget, scheduling date nights to ensure you stay connected, or simply taking ten minutes each day to share your high and low points.

Navigating marriage requires a blend of grace, effort, and a whole lot of love—fueled by a deep commitment to living out God's principles in your shared life. Each day offers a new opportunity to sow seeds of kindness, understanding, and support, cultivating a relationship that reflects God's love and stands firm in the face of life's inevitable challenges. By rooting your marriage in the fertile soil of God's Word, you ensure that, come what may, your union can grow, flourish, and bear fruit for years to come.

7.4 REBUILDING AFTER DIVORCE: EMBRACING PEACE AND REDISCOVERING SELF-WORTH

In the aftermath of a divorce, life can feel like navigating a stormy sea, with waves of emotions threatening to capsize your sense of self and peace. However, this challenging season can also be an opportunity for profound personal and spiritual growth. Much like a gardener tending to a neglected plot, you can cultivate a life of beauty and harmony by nurturing your well-being and embracing God's healing presence.

Biblical Perspectives on Healing

Divorce is undoubtedly a painful experience, but the Bible offers numerous examples of God's redemptive power in times of distress. Take comfort in Psalm 34:18, "The Lord is close to the brokenhearted and saves those who are crushed in spirit." This verse reassures you that God is ever-present, offering solace and strength during your most challenging moments. Reflecting on such scriptures can help shift your focus from the pain of the past to the promise of a hopeful future.

Scripture is filled with stories of individuals who faced significant life changes and emerged stronger in their faith. Consider Ruth, who, after losing her husband, chose to follow Naomi and embrace a new life in a foreign land. Her loyalty and faithfulness were rewarded, ultimately leading her to become the great-grand-mother of King David. Ruth's story demonstrates that even after profound loss, God's plan can bring unexpected blessings and new beginnings.

Another powerful example is found in the story of Hagar. Aban-doned and despairing in the wilderness, she encountered God, who provided for her and promised a future for her son. In Genesis 16:13, Hagar calls Him "El Roi," the God who sees me. This encounter reminds us that even in our darkest times, God sees our struggles and offers His unwavering support and guidance.

Embracing Self-Acceptance Through Faith

Self-acceptance is a crucial step in finding peace after divorce. Romans 8:1 reminds us, "Therefore, there is now no condemna-tion for those who are in Christ Jesus." This powerful message affirms that you are free from guilt and shame through Christ's redemption. Embracing this truth allows you to move forward with compassion for yourself, shedding the weight of self-criti-cism and regret.

Going through a divorce can trigger toxic thoughts such as "I'm a failure," "I will never be loved again," or "I'm not good enough." These negative beliefs can deeply impact self-esteem and spiritual well-being. Thoughts like "I'm a failure" often stem from societal pressures and personal expectations, leading to feelings of inade-quacy. Believing "I will never be loved again" can arise from rejec-tion and fear of the future, fostering hopelessness. Similarly, "I'm not good enough" can be rooted in past criticisms or guilt, causing you to doubt your value and worth.

Engaging in Christian contemplation can also facilitate this journey of self-acceptance. As you practice deep reflection and prayer, you invite God's presence into your healing process. This spiritual practice helps you reconnect with your true identity in Christ, fostering a sense of peace and purpose that transcends your circumstances. By meditating on scriptures that affirm God's love and promises, such as Jeremiah 29:11, which assures, "For I know the plans I have for you," declares the Lord, "plans to prosper you and not to harm you, plans to give you hope and a future," you can begin to dismantle the lies that have taken root in your mind.

Rebuilding and Moving Forward

Rebuilding your life after divorce involves practical steps and a commitment to personal growth. Surround yourself with a supportive community, whether through church groups, trusted friends, or professional counseling. Engaging in activities that nurture your body, mind, and spirit—such as exercise, creative pursuits, and volunteering—can also provide a sense of purpose and fulfillment.

Proverbs 3:5-6 encourages, "Trust in the Lord with all your heart and lean not on your own understanding; in all your ways submit to him, and he will make your paths straight." Trusting God's guidance is essential as you navigate this new chapter of your life. Allow His wisdom to direct your steps, and remain open to the possibilities He places before you.

Cultivating a Future of Peace and Fulfillment

Finding peace and self-acceptance after divorce is a journey of faith, resilience, and rediscovery. By embracing your identity in Christ and leaning on His promises, you can transform this challenging experience into an opportunity for growth and renewal. Each day is a step towards healing, a chance to cultivate a life that reflects God's love and grace. Remember that you are never alone; God walks with you, offering strength and hope for a brighter future.

Embrace this season as a time to invest deeply in your relationship with God, to serve with undivided attention, and to grow into the person He has called you to be. Take heart and dive deep into this journey, trusting that God will use this time to bring about new blessings and opportunities beyond what you could imagine. Your post-divorce years can be some of your life's most enriching and fulfilling seasons if you approach them with faith, purpose, and a spirit of adventure.

7.5 PARENTING WITH PATIENCE: STRESS MANAGEMENT TECHNIQUES FOR MOTHERS

Parenting mirrors the delicate art of sculpting, demanding constant focus, unwavering commitment, and a deep reservoir of patience, particularly in moments of challenge, such as when your child decides to turn breakfast into an impromptu art project across the room. Melding patience, scriptural wisdom, and a robust support network transforms the motherhood journey into an exquisite sculpture, carefully shaped and thriving under careful attention.

Scriptural Wisdom for Parents

Let's ground our parenting approach in the wisdom of Proverbs 22:6, which teaches, "Train up a child in the way he should go; even when he is old, he will not depart from it." This verse is not merely a directive to guide our children rightly; it's a reassuring promise that our efforts in shaping their paths are valuable investments in their futures. By instilling moral values, discipline, and a sense of purpose, we lay a foundation to influence their decisions and actions throughout their lives. This scripture encourages parents to be intentional and consistent in their guidance, knowing their efforts will impact their children's lives, fostering resilience and a solid moral compass.

Likewise, Colossians 3:21 warns, "Fathers, do not embitter your children, or they will become discouraged." This offers a critical insight into the impact of our words and deeds on our children's inner beings. It emphasizes the importance of nurturing our children with patience and understanding rather than harshness or excessive criticism. When we embitter our children, we risk diminishing their self-worth and motivation. This verse serves as a reminder to foster an environment of encouragement and support where children feel valued and understood. Balancing discipline with empathy helps prevent discouragement and promotes healthy emotional development.

Together, these scriptures illuminate the path forward: leading with a balance of truth and love, creating boundaries while nurturing the heart and spirit of our children with compassion and empathy. By integrating these principles, parents can cultivate a nurturing environment where children feel secure, respected, and inspired to grow into their best selves. This holistic approach to parenting, grounded in scriptural wisdom, guides children towards righteousness and strengthens the parent-child relationship, building a foundation of trust and mutual respect that endures through all stages of life.

Patience-Building Practices

So, how does one cultivate the kind of patience that not only endures but empowers? It starts within. Here is an example. When tensions rise—perhaps during a homework battle or a bedtime standoff—try taking a deep breath and silently reciting Philippians 4:13, "I can do all things through Christ who strengthens me." This moment of tapping into the Spirit of Christ inside you can recalibrate your emotions, reminding you of your strength in Christ, even in the face of parenting challenges.

Another powerful tool is prayer focused on patience. Each morning, or in those challenging moments, take a minute to pray for the Holy Spirit to fill your day with peace and patience. Ask God to help you see your children through His eyes, particularly when patience wears thin. Additionally, seek God's wisdom to tackle challenging situations. James 1:5 encourages us, "If any of you lacks wisdom, you should ask God, who gives generously to all without finding fault, and it will be given to you." This ensures that you are not relying solely on your understanding but seeking divine guidance to navigate parenting challenges effectively.

These spiritual practices foster patience and deepen your reliance on God's strength rather than your own. By integrating scripture, prayer, and seeking divine wisdom into your daily routine, you can cultivate a patience that empowers, strengthens, and enhances your ability to parent with grace and compassion. This approach transforms your reactions and sets a powerful example for your children, demonstrating the importance of relying on God in all aspects of life.

Balancing Parenting and Personal Time

Maintaining your spiritual health is vital, not just for you, but for the little eyes watching how you balance life's demands. It's essential to carve out time for your spiritual nourishment—be it through daily devotionals, prayer time, or simply moments of silent meditation. This isn't selfish; it's necessary. A spiritually fulfilled mom is equipped to pour love, wisdom, and patience into her parenting. If finding time seems impossible, consider integrating spiritual practices into your family routine. For example, you could start a family devotional where everyone shares something they're thankful for or read a Bible story together before bed. This not only feeds your spirit but also models a life of faith to your children.

Also, don't shy away from setting aside time for self-care. Whether it's a quiet coffee before the kids wake up, a brisk walk in the afternoon, or a book at bedtime, these small acts of self-care can reset and rejuvenate your spirit. Remember, you can't pour from an empty cup. Nurturing yourself is vital to nurturing your family.

Support Networks for Mothers

Nobody should navigate motherhood alone. Engaging with church groups or community initiatives that support mothers can be incredibly enriching. Many churches offer moms' groups or parenting classes that provide both fellowship and practical resources for managing the stresses of parenthood. These groups can be a great place to find mentorship, share challenges, and glean wisdom from other moms who've walked the path before you.

In essence, parenting with patience is less about mastering control and more about mastering the art of surrender—surrender to God's timing, His strength, and His way of doing things. It's about embracing the truth that every day may not be perfect, but every day, there is an opportunity to plant seeds of patience, love, and faith that will grow into something beautiful in your and your children's lives. So take heart, breathe deep, and lean on the timeless wisdom of scripture, the renewing grace of personal time, and the supportive arms of community to guide you through the rewarding, sometimes rocky, always worthwhile adventure of motherhood.

7.6 DEALING WITH LOSS AND GRIEF: COMFORTING SCRIPTURES AND PRACTICES

Walking through grief can feel like moving through a thick fog—confused, isolated, and unsure of what comes next. During these challenging times, when our hearts are heavy, and we can't see the path ahead, the Scriptures shine as a beacon of hope and comfort. These holy texts have provided solace and strength throughout history and hold profound truths to guide us out of the shadows. Psalm 34:18 brings us deep comfort, proclaiming, "The Lord is close to the brokenhearted and saves those who are crushed in spirit," reminding us that this isn't just moving language but a declaration of God's nearness in our pain. Similarly, Revelation 21:4 offers a vision of a future free from sorrow, where there is no death, mourning, or pain, under God's loving rule. These passages serve as a balm for our sorrowful hearts, reassuring us of God's constant presence and the hope for eternal serenity.

Grief as a Community Journey

The body of Christ is designed not just for Sunday worship but for supporting its members through life's most challenging times. One of the most tangible ways this support manifests is through the ministry of presence—simply being there for those who grieve. This doesn't require grand gestures; often, it's your presence that speaks volumes more than any words could. Churches can organize meal trains, where members provide meals to the grieving family, easing their daily burdens. Prayer vigils can be a powerful way to surround the grieving with love and intercession, making the journey through grief a shared rather than solitary one.

Moreover, many churches offer or can connect individuals with grief counseling and support groups. These groups provide a safe space to share your grief journey with others who understand the unique pain of loss. Here, amidst shared stories and collective tears, healing often begins. It's about creating a community buffer around the raw edges of grief, providing strength to navigate through the pain.

The presence of a caring community not only offers practical help but also emotional solace, reducing the feelings of isolation that can amplify anxiety and depression. Sharing the burden of grief with others who care creates a sense of belonging and understanding, which is essential for mental health and well-being. By fostering a community that actively supports its grieving members, the church plays a crucial role in promoting healing and resilience, helping individuals navigate their grief with the comfort of knowing they are not alone.

Rituals and Memorials

Christian practices and rituals can significantly aid in the grieving process, helping to externalize internal sorrow and commemorate the lives of loved ones. Memorial services, for instance, are not just about saying goodbye; they are ceremonies of remembrance, celebrating the life that was lived and the impact it made. These services, infused with scriptural readings and prayer, can offer immense comfort, reminding us of the hope of resurrection and eternal life that frames our earthly farewells.

Another profound practice is creating memory books or boxes. This can be a beautifully therapeutic activity where you compile photos, notes, and mementos that celebrate the deceased's life. Engaging in this act allows you to reminisce, reflect, and even find joy in the memories of the times shared. It's a way of honoring the past relationship while processing the loss, stitching together the fragments of memory into a tapestry of continued love and legacy.

As you navigate the complexities of grief, remember you are not walking this path alone. The scriptures provide a foundation of comfort and hope, the community offers its collective strength, and the rituals and memorials allow us to honor and remember those we've lost. In all these, the love of God acts as both anchor and compass, guiding us through the storm toward a horizon where peace waits with open arms. So hold tight to these truths, lean on your community, and let each step, no matter how small, carry you forward toward healing and hope.

7.7 FACING INFERTILITY: SUPPORT, HOPE, AND HEALING IN SCRIPTURE

Infertility is a profoundly challenging experience that affects many individuals and couples, bringing with it a unique blend of emotional and spiritual trials. The longing for a child and the repeated disappointments can lead to feelings of isolation, grief, and despair. During these difficult times, the Bible provides comfort and strength. It contains numerous stories of individuals who faced similar struggles and found hope and healing through their faith. These scriptural accounts offer valuable lessons and reassurance, reminding us that we are not alone in our journey and that God's plans for us are filled with love and purpose.

Emotional and Spiritual Impacts of Infertility

Navigating the challenges of infertility can often feel like a solitary journey, filled with a complex array of emotions, including deep yearning and profound grief, accompanied by a mix of other confusing feelings. Amidst this emotional turmoil, it's common to experience feelings of inadequacy and frustration, leading to questions about why this difficult path has been laid before you.

During these moments of vulnerability, scripture offers solace and assurance, affirming that our worth and purpose extend far beyond our capacity for childbearing and are deeply rooted in God's boundless love. Psalm 113:9 shines a beacon of hope, proclaiming, "He gives the barren woman a home, making her the joyous mother of children. Praise the Lord." This passage is a hopeful reminder of God's ability to fill voids with abundance and invites us to find joy and contentment in the present, trusting in His ultimate plan and perfect timing.

Stories of Biblical Figures Who Faced Infertility

The Bible doesn't shy away from the topic of infertility; instead, it presents it with raw honesty through the stories of women like Sarah, Rachel, and Hannah. Each of these women experienced the ache of empty arms, and each story is a testament to the fact that while God's plans may test us, they never aim to break us. Take Hannah, for instance, whose tearful prayers in 1 Samuel 1 reveal a woman wrestling with profound grief. Yet, her story unfolds to not just motherhood but to birthing a prophet who would anoint kings.

These narratives are not fairy tales but factual accounts of women in ancient times who echo the struggles many face today. They teach us about patience, endurance, and the transformative power of faith, reminding us that sometimes, the most significant victories come from the hardest battles.

Guide on Finding and Offering Support

If this is your current journey, look for support groups within your church or community. These groups can be safe havens where you can share your story, listen to others, and find comfort in not walking alone. For church communities, offering support might mean organizing specific prayer groups or informational sessions about infertility and providing spiritual and practical support. Being open about this struggle can break down the walls of isolation, building a community tapestry of support and understanding.

For those looking to support loved ones facing infertility, remember that often, the best support is your presence and a listening ear. Job's friends in the Bible initially just sat with him in his suffering—sometimes, the ministry of presence is the most powerful. Offer to pray with and for them, not just for the blessing of a child but for strength, peace, and understanding through the journey.

Exploration of All Options

In the quest to grow a family, there are many paths up the mountain—some choose to pursue treatments like IVF, others explore adoption, and some might look into foster care. Each option carries its own set of emotional and spiritual considerations. Faith doesn't prescribe a one-size-fits-all answer but offers a compass for navigating these decisions. It's about seeking God's guidance through prayer, consulting with trusted spiritual and medical counselors, and considering what path aligns with your values and circumstances.

Jeremiah 29:11 reassures us, "For I know the plans I have for you, declares the Lord, plans for welfare and not for evil, to give you a future and a hope." Whether your journey to parenthood takes a traditional route or an unexpected turn, this verse reminds us that every step is woven into the larger tapestry of His plan for your life.

Experiencing infertility means moving between moments of profound sorrow and peaks of hopeful anticipation, sometimes simultaneously. Scripture and fellowship provide not only avenues for support but also deep wells of fortitude.

Every biblical story, every scripture, and every moment of shared vulnerability and intercession strengthens the fabric of our faith and resilience. This collective journey reminds us that in our most desolate times, we are unequivocally accompanied.

7.8 NAVIGATING LIFE TRANSITIONS: SCRIPTURAL INSIGHTS FOR MAJOR DECISIONS

Have you ever stood at a crossroads, every path promising new adventures but also new challenges? Life is chock-full of these transition periods—moving cities, changing careers, starting a family, or redefining personal goals. These moments can stir up a cocktail of excitement and anxiety, hope and uncertainty. But here's the kicker: you should not navigate these choppy waters alone! Scripture is your compass, packed with divine wisdom waiting to guide you. For instance, James 1:5 encourages us to ask God for wisdom without doubting, and He promises to give generously. Meanwhile, Proverbs 3:5- 6 nudges us to trust in the Lord with all our hearts and lean not on our own understanding; in all our ways, submit to Him, and He will make our paths straight. These practical verses offer clear direction that can light the way as you step into the unknown.

Biblical Guidance for Decision-Making

The Bible serves as a reliable blueprint for decision-making. Take Proverbs 16:3, which advises us to commit our work to the Lord, and our plans will be established. This doesn't mean a passive approach to planning; instead, it's about aligning our desires with divine purpose, ensuring that our decisions are not just good but God-led. It's a reminder to involve God in every decision, consulting Him through prayer, scripture, and the wise counsel of fellow believers. This proactive spiritual alignment helps ensure that your choices are feasible and fruitful, leading to outcomes that glorify God and fulfill your God-given potential.

Prayer Models for Seeking Guidance

Think of prayer as your direct line to divine guidance, a conversation where you speak but also pause to listen.

Here's a practical approach:

1. Start with thanksgiving by acknowledging God's past faithfulness because remembering His guidance can bolster your confidence in His future help.
2. Then, present your specific requests. Be honest about your hopes, fears, and the decisions you face. Ask for clarity and peace, which, as Philippians 4:7 explains, will guard your heart and mind.
3. Finally, practice silence. Listening for God's response isn't about expecting an audible reply but sensing His guidance through a scripture that suddenly seems relevant, advice from a friend that resonates unexpectedly, or having peace about a particular decision path.

This dynamic prayer model keeps your heart attuned to divine whispers, even amid life's loudest transitions.

Utilizing Spiritual Community for Support

Who says you have to figure it all out on your own? Your church family, small groups, and spiritual mentors are invaluable resources. Let's say you're contemplating a job change or moving to a new city; why not leverage your community's collective wisdom and spiritual discernment? Acts 15:28 shows us how the early church made decisions not in isolation but through consultation and agreement within the community, seeking what seemed good to the Holy Spirit and them. This communal approach to decision-making can provide a broader perspective, helping you see angles you might otherwise miss. It's about enriching your decision-making process with communal prayer, shared insights, and the supportive strength of fellowship, making the journey through transitions not just bearable but enriching. Proverbs 11:14 reminds us, "There is safety in the multitude of counselors."

As you face your crossroads, remember that each decision is an opportunity to deepen your trust in God's plan, strengthen your spiritual roots, and expand your faith horizons. Embrace these transitions not with trepidation but with confidence, knowing that the same God who leads you is the God who loves you. With scripture as your guide, prayer as your practice, and community as your support system, you're well-equipped to navigate any change life throws your way. Let these tools shape your journey, and watch as each step becomes a testimony of trust, leading you to new places and heights in your spiritual walk.

Let's carry forward this spirit of guided resilience, ready to face not just life's changes but its challenges and celebrations, all under the umbrella of God's sovereign plan.

CHAPTER 8 SCRIPTURES TO SHUT UP SPECIFIC TOXIC THOUGHTS

"All Scripture is God-breathed and is useful for teaching, rebuking, correcting and training in righteousness, so that the servant of God may be thoroughly equipped for every good work."

— *2 TIMOTHY 3:16-17*

This chapter is your go-to guide for flipping the script on those lies with the powerful truth found in God's Word. By anchoring yourself in these scriptural truths, you're not just countering negative thoughts but cultivating a mindset rooted in divine value and hope. Each verse you memorize, each affirmation you declare, and each reflection you ponder doesn't just push back the darkness—it lights up your world, guiding you to live fully and freely as the cherished, purposeful creation you are.

So, keep these scriptures close. Write them on your heart, stick them on your fridge, or set them as your phone wallpaper. Let them constantly remind you that you are priceless in God's eyes. And in this truth, find the strength to rise above the lies and embrace the beautiful reality of who you are in Him.

8.1 VERSES THAT UPLIFT: BATTLING FEELINGS OF WORTHLESSNESS

- Psalm 139:14, "I praise you because I am fearfully and wonderfully made; your works are wonderful, I know that full well."

King David, who despite his royal status, had his fair share of down-and-out days. When he speaks of being "fearfully and wonderfully made," he's not bragging; he's proclaiming his awe at being a creation of God, flaws and all!

- Jeremiah 29:11, "For I know the plans I have for you," declares the LORD, "plans to prosper you and not to harm you, plans to give you hope and a future."

This scripture was written in a letter to the exiles in Babylon, people forcibly removed from their homes and struggling with loss and uncertainty. This verse offered them a lifeline of hope— that their current struggles were not the end of their story.

- Nehemiah 8:10, "The joy of the Lord is my strength."

This is an all-time favorite for when you need a boost in your mood and energy. It emphasizes that true strength and resilience come from the joy and comfort found in a relationship with God. This joy, rooted in God's presence and promises, empowers believers to face challenges with confidence and hope.

Personal Reflection Prompts

To deepen your engagement with these scriptures, reflect on how they relate to your life. Ask yourself, "When do I feel most worthless, and how can reminding myself that I am 'wonderfully made' counteract those feelings?" or "What hopes and plans am I holding onto that align with Jeremiah 29:11?" Write your thoughts and answers in a journal. Allow these truths to saturate your mind and spirit, transforming your self-view from the inside out.

8.2 OVERCOMING FEAR AND ANXIETY IN DAILY LIFE

- Isaiah 41:10, "So do not fear, for I am with you; do not be dismayed, for I am your God. I will strengthen you and help you; I will uphold you with my righteous right hand."

Isaiah doesn't just tell you not to fear; it reassures you that you're not alone. The phrase "I am with you" is a gentle yet powerful reminder that God isn't a distant observer; He's an active participant in your struggles. And when He says, "I will uphold you," imagine the strongest, most secure grip that never tires or weakens —that's the kind of support being promised.

- 2 Timothy 1:7, "For God has not given us a spirit of fear, but of power and of love and of a sound mind."
- 1 Peter 5:7, "Cast all your anxiety on Him because He cares for you."
- Philippians 4:6-7, "Do not be anxious about anything, but in every situation, by prayer and petition, with thanksgiving, present your requests to God. And the peace of God, which transcends all understanding, will guard your hearts and your minds in Christ Jesus."

These passages offer a step-by-step guide to peace. It starts by redirecting our instinct to worry into an invitation to communicate with God openly and gratefully. The promise that follows is the kind of peace that doesn't just calm but also protects— guarding hearts and minds like a vigilant, loving sentinel. For instance, when you feel overwhelmed, pray, "Lord, I'm handing over my fears to you just like Philippians 4:6-7 says. Please let your peace guard my heart and mind." Make these scriptures your go-to dialogue with God.

- Psalm 23, "The Lord is my shepherd, I lack nothing. He makes me lie down in green pastures; he leads me beside quiet waters; he refreshes my soul. He guides me along the right paths for his name's sake. Even though I walk through the darkest valley, I will fear no evil, for you are with me; your rod and your staff, they comfort me. You prepare a table before me in the presence of my enemies. You anoint my head with oil; my cup overflows. Surely your goodness and love will follow me all the days of my life, and I will dwell in the house of the Lord forever."

Psalm 23 is a classic go-to for anyone needing reassurance of God's guidance and care.

- Psalm 34:4, "I sought the Lord, and he answered me; he delivered me from all my fears."
- Psalm 94:19, "When anxiety was great within me, your consolation brought joy to my soul."
- Psalm 16:8, "I keep my eyes always on the Lord. With him at my right hand, I will not be shaken."
- Psalm 127:1: "Unless the Lord builds the house, the builders labor in vain."

Psalm 127 reminds us that without God's guidance and blessing, our efforts are ultimately futile. It emphasizes the importance of relying on God in all our endeavors, recognizing that true success and stability come only through His involvement and support.

- Exodus 33:14, "My presence will go with you, and I will give you rest."

Techniques for Meditative Reading

Meditative reading, or lectio divina, is a beautiful way to let the Psalms sink from your head into your heart. Start by selecting a Psalm. Read it slowly, aloud, if possible, allowing each word to resonate. Pause whenever a phrase or verse strikes you, and dwell on it, turning it over in your mind. Ask yourself what God might be saying to you through these words. This shouldn't be a rush to the finish; it's about letting the divine whisper echo in the chambers of your soul. If distractions come, gently guide your focus back to the words, just as you might gently redirect a puppy back to its yard. This practice can transform your reading time from a routine to a rich dialogue with God.

As you weave these verses into the fabric of your daily life, they become more than just words; they become anchors. Whether whispered in a moment of panic, prayed over in the morning, or shared with a friend in need, these scriptures stand ready to guide you back to peace.

So, the next time fear or anxiety tries to derail your day, reach for these divine assurances and remember: with God's Word in your heart, you have everything you need to face whatever comes your way.

8.3 HANDLING CRITICISM AND REJECTION

Even the most celebrated figures in the Bible faced their share of naysayers and door slammers. As uncomfortable as these experiences are, they come with a hidden gift—resilience. The Scriptures will help you endure criticism and rejection and grow stronger through them.

- Proverbs 29:25, "Fear of man will prove to be a snare, but whoever trusts in the Lord is kept safe."

It reminds us that relying on human approval and fearing others can trap and hinder us. Instead, placing our trust in the Lord provides proper security and protection, freeing us from the constraints of seeking validation from people.

- Matthew 5:11-12, "Blessed are you when people insult you, persecute you, and falsely say all kinds of evil against you because of me. Rejoice and be glad because great is your reward in heaven..."

Here, Christ doesn't just acknowledge our suffering; He reframes it as a cause for joy and a source of divine reward, turning the sting of rejection into a badge of honor.

Analyzing Biblical Examples:

Nehemiah: Rebuilding the Walls of Jerusalem

Nehemiah, a Jewish cupbearer to the Persian king Artaxerxes, learned that Jerusalem's walls were in ruins and its gates burned. Deeply moved, he sought the king's permission to return to Jerusalem and rebuild its walls. With the king's blessing, Nehemiah embarked on this daunting task. However, he faced significant criticism and rejection from local leaders such as Sanballat, Tobiah, and Geshem, who mocked and ridiculed his efforts. Despite their opposition, Nehemiah remained resolute. He organized the people, prayed for God's help, and continued the work undeterred. Nehemiah's perseverance and reliance on God enabled him to complete the wall in just 52 days (Nehemiah 1-6).

His story teaches us several valuable lessons on handling criticism and rejection:

- Prayer and Dependence on God: Nehemiah consistently turned to prayer when faced with opposition. He sought divine guidance and strength to persevere.
- Focus on the Mission: Nehemiah stayed focused on his mission. Despite the ridicule and threats, he did not let criticism distract him from his goal.
- Leadership and Encouragement: Nehemiah inspired and organized the people, encouraging them to work together despite the challenges. He demonstrated strong leadership in the face of adversity.
- Perseverance: Nehemiah's determination to see the project through despite ongoing opposition highlights the importance of perseverance.

Jesus: Rejection at Nazareth

When Jesus began his ministry, he returned to his hometown of Nazareth and taught in the synagogue. Initially, the people were amazed at his wisdom and miraculous powers. However, their amazement quickly turned to skepticism and rejection. They questioned his authority, saying, "Isn't this the carpenter's son? Isn't his mother's name Mary, and aren't his brothers James, Joseph, Simon, and Judas?" (Matthew 13:55). Feeling too familiar with him and offended by his claims, they rejected him, and Jesus responded by stating, "A prophet is not without honor except in his own town and in his own home." Despite their rejection, Jesus continued his ministry, performing few miracles there due to their lack of faith (Matthew 13:54-58, Luke 4:16-30).

Jesus' experience in Nazareth provides critical insights into handling criticism and rejection:

- Acceptance of Reality: Jesus recognized rejection as part of the prophetic calling, especially among those familiar with us. He did not let this deter him from his mission.
- Maintain Composure and Integrity: Despite facing rejection from those who knew him best, Jesus maintained his composure and integrity. He did not respond with anger or frustration.
- Continued Focus on Mission: Jesus did not allow the rejection in Nazareth to halt his ministry. He continued teaching and healing in other towns where people were more receptive.
- Faith in the Bigger Picture: Jesus understood that rejection by some did not invalidate his mission or message. He kept faith in God's plan and continued his work despite local opposition.

Both Nehemiah and Jesus provide powerful examples of handling criticism and rejection with grace and perseverance. Nehemiah's reliance on prayer, focus, leadership, and perseverance enabled him to overcome opposition and achieve his goal. Jesus' acceptance of reality, composure, continued focus, and faith in God's plan highlight how to remain steadfast in the face of rejection.

These stories teach us that criticism and rejection are inevitable but can be navigated with faith, determination, and a clear sense of purpose. Incorporating biblical principles into your response to these challenges can serve as a barricade against the emotional distress that often undermines our mental health.

Strategies for Resilience

Building resilience against criticism and rejection starts with internalizing the truths of Scripture. It's about letting these truths soak into your bones until they become part of who you are. When criticism comes, counter it with affirmations of your identity in Christ, such as "I am fearfully and wonderfully made" or "I am a child of God." Practicing this kind of scriptural affirmation helps fortify your spiritual armor, making you less susceptible to the arrows of human judgment.

Another critical strategy is to maintain a heavenly perspective. Much like Jesus, who endured the cross "for the joy set before him," focusing on the eternal can help you handle the temporal pains of rejection. This doesn't mean ignoring your feelings but rather framing them within a larger, divine narrative. It's about seeing beyond the moment to the bigger picture of God's plan for your life, which includes using your experiences, both good and bad, for your ultimate good and His glory.

Opportunities Not Obstacles

In embracing these scriptural truths and strategies, remember that each challenge to your worth or calling isn't just an obstacle; it's an opportunity to deepen your faith, refine your character, and witness the sustaining power of God's Word in your life. These experiences also provide a powerful testimony to the grace and power of God, demonstrating His faithfulness and strength in your journey. So, the next time you face criticism or feel the sting of rejection, reach for these scriptural remedies and watch as they transform not only your perspective but also your heart.

8.4 GOD'S PROMISES ON PROVISION: COUNTERING FINANCIAL ANXIETY

When the bank balance isn't smiling back at you, these scriptures are a soothing balm.

- Philippians 4:19 says, "And my God will meet all your needs according to the riches of his glory in Christ Jesus."

Notice, it doesn't say 'might meet' or 'could meet'—it's a firm 'will meet.' This promise isn't based on the fluctuating economy or your current job status; it's anchored in the unchangeable richness of God's glory and His ability to provide.

- Matthew 6:31-33, "So do not worry, saying, 'What shall we eat?' or 'What shall we drink?' or 'What shall we wear?' For the pagans run after all these things, and your heavenly Father knows that you need them. But seek first his kingdom and his righteousness, and all these things will be given to you as well."

Here, Jesus addresses the common human concerns about basic needs and offers a profound assurance about God's provision. He urges his followers not to worry about their material needs—such as food, drink, and clothing—emphasizing that such anxiety is characteristic of those who do not know God ("the pagans"). Jesus reassures us that our heavenly Father is fully aware of our needs and is committed to providing for them.

The key to overcoming financial anxiety lies in prioritizing our relationship with God. Jesus instructs us to "seek first his kingdom and his righteousness." This means living according to God's will, pursuing spiritual growth, and aligning our lives with His purposes. When we prioritize our spiritual well-being and trust in God's provision, we are promised that "all these things will be given to you as well." This highlights the importance of faith and trust in God's provision, encouraging us to rely on Him rather than be consumed by worry about our material needs.

Theological Insights

To fully grasp the biblical perspective on provision, it's essential to draw a clear line between worldly wealth and spiritual abundance. The secular world often measures wealth in terms of monetary value and material possessions, suggesting that happiness and security are found in the accumulation of such assets. However, the Bible unfolds a more comprehensive and fulfilling understanding of provision, one that transcends mere physical sustenance. God's provision is all-encompassing, addressing our tangible needs and nurturing our emotional resilience and spiritual vitality. He is intimately aware of our needs, often before we even articulate them, and He commits to fulfilling them not because we have earned His benevolence but purely from His boundless generosity and love.

This divine approach to provision encourages us to shift our perspective from one of scarcity—fixating on our deficits and what we lack—to one of sufficiency and abundance in Christ. It invites us to view our lives through the lens of what we possess in Christ—peace, hope, and a lasting security that cannot be eroded by economic downturns or financial crises. By doing so, we learn to value the imperishable riches of God's kingdom over the fleeting wealth of the world, cultivating a heart of gratitude and trust in God's unfailing provision.

Application in Daily Life

Applying these promises to your everyday financial concerns involves a mix of practical stewardship and spiritual trust. Begin by assessing your financial habits. Are you spending wisely? Are you saving? Are you tithing? Are you giving? Aligning these practices with biblical stewardship principles can help ensure you manage God's provisions faithfully. Then, deepen your trust in God's promise to provide. This doesn't mean sitting back and waiting for a windfall. Instead, it's about doing your part—budgeting, working, saving—while trusting God to bless your efforts and fill in the gaps. It's recognizing that your security doesn't come from the numbers in your bank account but from your relationship with the One who owns the cattle on a thousand hills.

Faith-Building Exercises

Strengthening your faith in God's provision can be both enlightening and uplifting. Start with a 'Provision Journal.' For a month, jot down every instance of God's provision, no matter how small. Maybe you found a great deal at the supermarket, or perhaps a friend treated you to coffee when you were low on cash. Documenting these moments can help you see the continuous thread of God's faithfulness weaving through your life.

Additionally, engage in 'What If' prayers. For each financial worry, turn it into a prayer. For example, "What if I can't pay this bill?" becomes, "God, I trust you to provide the means to cover all my expenses." This practice brings your anxieties to God and reinforces your trust in His ability to meet every need.

As you embrace these scriptures and integrate these practices into your life, you'll find that financial anxiety loses its grip. Your confidence will grow not because your economic situation has necessarily changed, but because your perspective has. You're no longer at the mercy of your monetary status but resting in the assurance of divine provision.

So next time the bills pile up or the bank account dwindles, remember these promises. With God as your provider, you have access to wealth that never diminishes and a peace that surpasses all economic understanding. Let this assurance guide you through each financial challenge, turning every worry into a reminder of His faithfulness and every need into an opportunity to witness His provision firsthand.

8.5 HEALING WORDS: SCRIPTURES THAT SPEAK TO PHYSICAL AND EMOTIONAL HEALTH

Our journey through life is like a road trip. Along the way, you encounter bumps, detours, and, occasionally, a flat tire. In moments like these, where do you turn for a quick fix or a bit of maintenance? For many believers, the answer lies in the healing words of Scripture, serving as both a spare tire and a navigation system guiding us back onto the right path.

- Exodus 15:26, "I am the LORD, who heals you."
- James 5:14-15, "Is anyone among you sick? Let them call the elders of the church to pray over them and anoint them with oil in the name of the Lord. And the prayer offered in faith will make the sick person well; the Lord will raise them up."
- Proverbs 3:7-8, "Do not be wise in your own eyes; fear the Lord and shun evil. This will bring health to your body and nourishment to your bones."
- Psalm 147:3, "He heals the brokenhearted and binds up their wounds."

- Isaiah 40:29-31, "He gives strength to the weary and increases the power of the weak. Even youths grow tired and weary, and young men stumble and fall, but those who hope in the Lord will renew their strength. They will soar on wings like eagles; they will run and not grow weary; they will walk and not be faint."
- Matthew 11:28-30, "Come to me, all you who are weary and burdened, and I will give you rest. Take my yoke upon you and learn from me, for I am gentle and humble in heart, and you will find rest for your souls. For my yoke is easy, and my burden is light."
- 3 John 1:2, "Dear friend, I pray that you may enjoy good health and that all may go well with you, even as your soul is getting along well."
- Proverbs 17:22, "A cheerful heart is good medicine, but a crushed spirit dries up the bones."
- Jeremiah 30:17, "But I will restore you to health and heal your wounds,' declares the Lord."

Interpretation for Today

In today's fast-paced world, where medical advancements seem to offer a pill for every ill, plus a pill for every side effect of the pill fixing the ill, these verses remind us of a more profound truth: our ultimate healer is not found in a pharmacy, but in the divine physician.

Exodus 15:26 is part of a broader narrative where God promises health as a covenant benefit, contingent upon obedience and trust in Him. It's not just about physical healing; it's about maintaining a lifestyle that aligns with His commands, often leading to better health.

James 5:14-15, on the other hand, emphasizes the community's role in the healing process—encouraging us to lean not only on God but also on the godly support around us. These scriptures bridge ancient wisdom with modern challenges, reminding us that while medicine is a blessing, prayer is powerful and essential.

Integrating Prayer and Medical Care

Balancing faith in divine healing with responsible health practices can sometimes feel like walking a tightrope. How do we honor God's power to heal while also respecting the gifts of knowledge and medicine He has provided through doctors and researchers? The key lies in seeing medical care as a complement to spiritual care, not a competitor.

Use prayer as your first line of defense—asking for guidance, wisdom, and healing. Then, seek medical advice as needed, viewing it as part of God's provision. When you receive treatment, pray over it. Ask God to bless the medicines, the hands of the doctors and nurses, and the processes you undergo. This approach does not diminish God's power but showcases His sovereignty over every aspect of our lives, including modern medicine.

Incorporating these healing scriptures into your life allows you to tap into a wellspring of divine support, whether dealing with a common cold or a chronic condition. Let them remind you of God's readiness to heal, His commandments that guide us towards healthier lives, and the community He provides to uplift us in prayer.

So, next time you feel under the weather, reach for these scriptures as readily as you might reach for a medicine bottle. Let them soothe your spirit and fortify your faith, reminding you that, no matter the ailment, your recovery is in the hands of a capable, compassionate Creator.

8.6 OVERCOMING DOUBT: AFFIRMATIONS OF FAITH AND STRENGTH

Whether in the stillness of a sleepless night or amidst the hustle of daily life, doubt can quietly creep into our minds, undermining our confidence in our faith, decisions, and vision for what lies ahead.

Identifying Sources of Doubt

Recognizing the sources of doubt is the first step in turning those whispers of uncertainty into shouts of faith. Doubt can sneak into our minds through various channels—past failures, fear of the unknown, or even through comparisons fostered by the highlight reels of social media. It thrives on isolation and misinformation, often distorting our perception of reality. By pinpointing these triggers, you can begin to address them directly. For instance, if comparing yourself to others on social media sparks doubt in your personal achievements and spiritual journey, it might be time to curate your feed or take periodic breaks to refocus on your own path without distraction.

Create Personal Affirmations

Crafting personal affirmations from scriptures can transform them from abstract ideas into tangible truths that impact our daily lives. An affirmation is essentially a way of consistently speaking God's truth over your life until it echoes louder than the voice of doubt. Begin by selecting scriptures that speak directly to the areas in which you face the most doubt. For example, if you doubt your worth or purpose, affirm, "I am created in God's image, designed for a unique purpose, and equipped with gifts that no one else possesses." Make these affirmations personal and present tense, asserting them as current and active realities in your life.

To craft these affirmations, start with a scripture, then personalize it into a statement you can easily remember and declare. Write it down, say it out loud, and repeat it until it feels less like a statement and more like a belief. This practice doesn't just fight off doubt; it cultivates the garden of your mind, allowing faith, confidence, and peace to flourish.

Scripture Arsenal to Counter Doubt

- James 1:5- 6, "If any of you lacks wisdom, let him ask of God, who gives to all liberally and without reproach, and it will be given to him. But let him ask in faith, with no doubting, for he who doubts is like a wave of the sea driven and tossed by the wind."

This passage encourages us to seek wisdom from God with confidence and faith. It underscores the importance of asking without doubt, as doubt leads to instability and uncertainty. Trusting God wholeheartedly is critical to receiving His guidance and wisdom. The book of James reminds us that a double-minded man is unstable in all his ways and receives nothing from the Lord, highlighting the necessity of unwavering faith (James 1:6-8).

Affirmation: "I trust in God's wisdom and guidance. I ask in faith, without doubt, knowing that He will provide the direction I need."

- Mark 9:23-24, "If you can'?" said Jesus. "Everything is possible for one who believes." Immediately, the boy's father exclaimed, "I do believe; help me overcome my unbelief!"

In this story, a father seeking healing for his son acknowledges his struggle with doubt and asks Jesus to help him overcome it. Jesus' response highlights that belief makes all things possible. This scripture shows that it's okay to seek help in overcoming doubt and that faith can lead to miraculous outcomes.

Affirmation: "I believe in the power of Jesus to make all things possible. Lord, help me overcome my unbelief and strengthen my faith."

- Matthew 21:21, Jesus replied, "Truly I tell you, if you have faith and do not doubt, not only can you do what was done to the fig tree, but also you can say to this mountain, 'Go, throw yourself into the sea,' and it will be done."

Jesus emphasizes the power of faith without doubt. He illustrates that unwavering faith can achieve seemingly impossible things, symbolized by moving a mountain. This verse encourages us to maintain strong faith in God's power and promises.

Affirmation: "With unwavering faith, I can overcome any obstacle. I trust in God's power to move mountains in my life."

- Proverbs 3:5- 6 says, "Trust in the Lord with all your heart and lean not on your own understanding; in all your ways submit to him, and he will make your paths straight."

Sometimes, your situation and possible solution do not make natural sense or add up. This proverb advises complete trust in God rather than relying on one's own understanding. By submitting to God in all things, we can overcome doubt and experience God's supernatural abilities at work in our natural lives.

Affirmation: "I trust in the Lord with all my heart. I lean not to my own understanding. I submit my ways to Him, knowing He will make my paths straight."

- Psalm 94:19, "When doubts filled my mind, your comfort gave me renewed hope and cheer."

This verse acknowledges the reality of doubt but highlights God's comfort as a source of renewed hope and joy. It reassures us that God's presence and comfort can help dispel doubt and restore confidence.

Affirmation: "Even when doubts fill my mind, God's comfort renews my hope and brings me joy. I trust in His presence and strength."

Maintaining a Routine

Consistency is vital in making affirmations a powerful tool against doubt. Incorporate them into your daily routine by starting your day with a spoken affirmation or turning to them during moments of uncertainty. Keep them visible—post them on your mirror, set them as reminders on your phone, or tuck them in your wallet. In moments of weakness or questioning, these affirmations serve as beacons of truth, guiding you back to a mindset anchored in faith and strength.

Moreover, consider pairing your affirmations with prayer, asking God to reinforce these truths in your heart and continually reveal His presence and power in your life. This practice not only combats doubt but also deepens your relationship with God, as you rely on His truth to define and direct your life.

By actively identifying sources of doubt, countering them with scriptural truths, crafting personal affirmations, and maintaining a routine of declaration, you can navigate through the fog of uncertainty with the light of faith guiding your path. Embrace these practices, and watch as the shadows of doubt get overtaken by the dawn of God's promises in your life. So go ahead, speak life over your doubts, and step forward in the strength and assurance of your faith, ready to face whatever comes your way with a heart firmly rooted in His unshakeable truths.

8.7 EMPOWERMENT THROUGH THE WORD: VERSES FOR PERSONAL AND PROFESSIONAL GROWTH

Imagine stepping into your workplace armed with your professional skills and divine empowerment that spurs you toward excellence, high performance, and superior results. Sounds pretty invincible. Well, the Bible isn't just a spiritual guide; it's also a treasure trove of wisdom for personal and professional growth packed with empowering scriptures that can elevate your career and your entire approach to success.

- Joshua 1:8, "Keep this Book of the Law always on your lips; meditate on it day and night, so that you may be careful to do everything written in it. Then you will be prosperous and successful."
- Colossians 3:23, "Whatever you do, work at it with all your heart, as working for the Lord, not for human masters."
- Ephesians 3:20 says, "Now to him who is able to do immeasurably more than all we ask or imagine, according to his power that is at work within us."

Here, Paul isn't merely encouraging a good work ethic; he's transforming our perspective on work, turning every task into an act of worship. These verses remind us that our careers and daily tasks are arenas where we can demonstrate our commitment to God's standards of excellence, not just human expectations.

Insights on Biblical Success

Success in the Bible looks quite different from the world's often superficial benchmarks. Biblical success is deeply rooted in character and obedience to God. It's about aligning our actions with God's will and finding satisfaction in His approval rather than just human accolades. For instance, biblical success involves humility, service to others, and integrity—qualities that may not headline a typical success seminar but are central to God's definition of a life well-lived. This perspective doesn't downplay achievement or ambition but frames them within a larger, more eternal context.

Applying Scripture to Career Goals

Incorporating these biblical principles into your professional life can be challenging and rewarding. It means doing your job excellently, not just to earn a paycheck or climb the corporate ladder, but as a way to honor God. This could look like maintaining integrity when the pressure's on to cut corners or choosing to serve your colleagues even when it might not advance your interests. It's about seeing your workplace as a field where you can sow seeds of faith through your actions and attitudes.

Consider setting goals that reflect professional advancement and spiritual and ethical growth. How can you bring more honesty, creativity, and kindness into your work environment? These aren't just nice add-ons; they're central to succeeding on God's terms.

Role Models from Scripture

The Bible is rich with examples of individuals who exemplified personal and professional growth.

Daniel: From Exile to Advisor

Daniel's story (Daniel 1-6) highlights his rise from a young Jewish exile to a respected advisor in the Babylonian and Persian empires.

Despite being in a foreign land and facing attempts to undermine his faith, Daniel consistently displayed wisdom, integrity, and an unwavering commitment to God. His excellence in his duties and ability to interpret dreams and visions earned him a prominent position and respect for multiple kings. Daniel's growth demonstrates the importance of faithfulness, wisdom, and maintaining one's principles, even in challenging environments.

Esther: From Orphan to Queen

Esther's journey (Esther 1-10) from an orphaned Jewish girl to the queen of Persia illustrates significant personal and professional growth. Faced with the threat of her people's annihilation, Esther bravely intervened by risking her own life to approach King Xerxes and reveal Haman's plot. Her courage, wisdom, and strategic thinking saved her people and secured her place in history as a heroine of faith. Esther's story demonstrates the impact of courage, strategic action, and the importance of using one's position for the greater good.

Lydia: From Merchant to Supporter of the Early Church

Lydia's story (Acts 16:11-15) exemplifies professional success and personal growth. Lydia was a successful businesswoman dealing with purple cloth. She was a prominent and independent woman in her community. When she encountered Paul and his companions, she accepted their message and became a believer. Lydia's home became a meeting place for Christians, and she provided crucial support for Paul's ministry. Her story highlights the importance of hospitality, generosity, and using one's resources to support the growth of the early church. Lydia's transformation shows how personal faith can influence professional life and have a broader impact on the community.

Overcoming Anxiety About Your Ability to Succeed

These biblical examples offer valuable lessons for countering stress and anxiety about one's ability to succeed in life:

1. Faith and Trust in God: Trusting in God's plan and timing, as Daniel, Esther, and Lydia did, can alleviate anxiety and provide a sense of purpose and direction. Believing that God is in control helps shift the focus from personal limitations to divine possibilities.
2. Perseverance and Resilience: Each of these individuals faced significant challenges and setbacks. Their stories remind us that growth often comes through overcoming difficulties and that perseverance is vital to personal and professional success.
3. Integrity and Excellence: Maintaining integrity and striving for excellence, regardless of circumstances, leads to recognition and success. Daniel's commitment to his values and Lydia's ethical business practices brought them favor and advancement.
4. Courage and Strategic Action: Esther's bravery in the face of potential death highlights the importance of courage and taking strategic actions. Facing fears and making bold decisions can lead to remarkable outcomes.
5. Generosity and Support: Lydia's use of her resources to support the early church illustrates the importance of generosity and community support. Success is not just personal but also involves contributing to the growth and well-being of others.

By applying these principles, you can navigate your path to success with greater confidence and less anxiety, knowing that growth is a process guided by faith, perseverance, integrity, courage, and generosity.

Incorporating these scriptural principles and examples into your life isn't about separating the secular from the spiritual; it's about integrating them. It's seeing every task, every challenge, and every opportunity at work as a chance to display the transformative power of living according to God's Word. So, as you move forward in your career, carry these scriptures and stories with you as reminders and guides. Let them shape what you do and how you do it, infusing your work with purpose, integrity, and a touch of the divine.

Remember, your professional life isn't a separate story from your spiritual journey—it's a pivotal part of the narrative God is writing in your life. Each scripture studied, each principle applied, and each example followed is a step toward embodying the success that God desires for you—one that enriches not just your bank account but also your soul and the lives of those around you.

8.8 THE LIES VERSUS THE TRUTH

Lies About Yourself

- "I'm too broken to be fixed."

Psalm 34:18, "The Lord is close to the brokenhearted and saves those who are crushed in spirit."

Psalm 147:3, "He heals the brokenhearted and binds up their wounds."

This verse reassures us that God can heal and restore us no matter how broken we may feel. It emphasizes God's compassion and ability to mend our hearts and lives. This promise of healing and restoration offers hope and encouragement, reminding us that there is no brokenness too great to be fixed with God.

- "I must be perfect."

James 3:2, "We all stumble in many ways."

It's a gentle reminder that stumbling isn't an anomaly; it's part of the human condition—a condition fully known and lovingly accepted by God.

- "I'm unlovable."

Romans 5:8, "But God demonstrates his own love for us in this: While we were still sinners, Christ died for us."

This scripture doesn't just suggest that God's love is unconditional; it declares it with the certainty of Christ's sacrifice. It's a love not predicated on us being lovable but rooted in His unchangeable nature.

- "I have no one. I'm all alone."

Hebrews 13:5: "Never will I leave you; never will I forsake you."

This verse reassures us that God is always with us, offering His unwavering presence and support. It emphasizes that we are never truly alone because God promises never to leave or forsake us. By trusting in God's constant companionship, we can find strength and courage, knowing we are always cared for and supported by Him.

- "I can't do this"

2 Corinthians 12:9, "My grace is sufficient for you, for my power is made perfect in weakness."

It's a divine paradox that turns our cultural understanding of strength and adequacy on its head—our weaknesses, in fact, are the perfect canvas for God's strength.

- "I'm not good enough."

Ephesians 2:10, "For we are God's handiwork, created in Christ Jesus to do good works, which God prepared in advance for us to do."

- "I'm a failure."

Jeremiah 29:11, "For I know the plans I have for you," declares the Lord, "plans to prosper you and not to harm you, plans to give you hope and a future."

This verse reminds us that God has a purposeful and prosperous plan for us, filled with hope and a bright future. It reassures us that our perceived failures are not the end of our story but rather a part of the journey God is using to shape and lead us toward His more excellent plans. This promise helps us see beyond our current struggles and trust God's good intentions for our lives.

- "I can continue to live in sin and not face consequences because God is good."

Galatians 6:7-8, "Do not be deceived: God cannot be mocked. A man reaps what he sows. Whoever sows to please their flesh, from the flesh will reap destruction; whoever sows to please the Spirit, from the Spirit will reap eternal life."

- "God doesn't love me."

1 John 4:9-10, "This is how God showed his love among us: He sent his one and only Son into the world that we might live through him. This is love: not that we loved God, but that he loved us and sent his Son as an atoning sacrifice for our sins."

Romans 8:35-39, "Who shall separate us from the love of Christ? Shall trouble or hardship or persecution or famine or nakedness or danger or sword? As it is written: "For your sake we face death all day long; we are considered as sheep to be slaughtered." No, in all these things, we are more than conquerors through him who loved us. For I am convinced that neither death nor life, neither angels nor demons, neither the present nor the future, nor any powers, neither height nor depth, nor anything else in all creation, will be able to separate us from the love of God that is in Christ Jesus our Lord."

- "I can't take this any longer."

1 Corinthians 10:13, "No temptation has overtaken you except what is common to mankind. And God is faithful; he will not let you be tempted beyond what you can bear. But when you are tempted, he will also provide a way out so that you can endure it."

This verse reassures us that God knows our struggles and will not allow us to face more than we can handle. It emphasizes God's faithfulness in providing us with the strength to endure and the means to overcome our difficulties. By trusting in God's promise, we can find hope and resilience, knowing that we are never alone and that He will always provide a way through our trials.

Lies About A Significant Other

- "They don't really care about me."

1 Corinthians 13:4-7, "Love is patient, love is kind. It does not envy, it does not boast, it is not proud. It does not dishonor others, it is not self-seeking, it is not easily angered, it keeps no record of wrongs. Love does not delight in evil but rejoices with the truth. It always protects, always trusts, always hopes, always perseveres."

- "I'm better off alone."

Ecclesiastes 4:9-10, "Two are better than one, because they have a good return for their labor: If either of them falls down, one can help the other up. But pity anyone who falls and has no one to help them up."

This passage highlights the importance and benefits of companionship and mutual support. It emphasizes that having someone by your side provides strength, assistance, and encouragement, especially during difficult times. This scripture reassures us that we are not meant to navigate life alone and that having supportive relationships is valuable and beneficial.

- "I will only be truly happy once I have a husband."

Psalm 16:11, "You make known to me the path of life; you will fill me with joy in Your presence, with eternal pleasures at your right hand."

This verse reminds us that true joy and fulfillment come from God's presence, not our marital status or any other earthly relationship. It emphasizes that God is the ultimate source of lasting happiness and contentment. By seeking fulfillment in our relationship with God, we can experience profound joy and peace, whether single or married.

- "My husband is responsible for my happiness."

Philippians 4:11-13, "I am not saying this because I am in need, for I have learned to be content whatever the circumstances. I know what it is to be in need, and I know what it is to have plenty. I have learned the secret of being content in any and every situation, whether well-fed or hungry, whether living in plenty or in want. I can do all this through him who gives me strength."

This passage emphasizes that true contentment comes from within and through our relationship with Christ rather than being dependent on external circumstances or other people. It teaches that we can find strength and fulfillment in Christ, who empowers us to be content in every situation. Relying on God for our happiness ensures a stable and lasting source of joy, independent of others.

Lies About Your Body

- "I'm ugly."

Genesis 1:27, "So God created mankind in his own image, in the image of God he created them; male and female he created them."

It reminds you that you are created in the image of God, reflecting His beauty and glory.

Psalm 139:14, "I praise you because I am fearfully and wonderfully made; your works are wonderful, I know that full well."

This verse emphasizes that we are intentionally and beautifully created by God. It affirms that every person is crafted with care and purpose, reflecting God's wonderful work. Recognizing that we are "fearfully and wonderfully made" helps us appreciate our inherent beauty and worth as God's creation, countering negative self-perceptions about our appearance.

Proverbs 31:30, "Charm is deceptive, and beauty is fleeting; but a woman who fears the Lord is to be praised."

1 Peter 3:3-4, "Your beauty should not come from outward adornments, such as elaborate hairstyles and the wearing of gold jewelry or fine clothes. Rather, it should be that of your inner self, the unfading beauty of a gentle and quiet spirit, which is of great worth in God's sight."

It encourages you to focus on the inner beauty that is precious to God.

Isaiah 64:8, "Yet you, Lord, are our Father. We are the clay, you are the potter; we are all the work of your hand."

Affirms that you are a carefully crafted masterpiece made by God.

Song of Solomon 4:7, "You are altogether beautiful, my darling; there is no flaw in you."

This verse celebrates your unique and flawless beauty as seen through God's eyes.

- "I'm fat/too skinny/butt too small/too big."

1 Samuel 16:7, "But the Lord said to Samuel, 'Do not consider his appearance or his height, for I have rejected him. The Lord does not look at the things people look at. People look at the outward appearance, but the Lord looks at the heart.'"

This verse highlights that God values the condition of our hearts more than our outward appearance. It reminds us that our worth is not determined by physical attributes but by our inner character and relationship with God. Understanding this truth can help us shift our focus from external insecurities to the qualities that truly matter, fostering a healthier and more positive self-image.

Lies About Your Parenting

- "I'm a bad mother."

Proverbs 22:6 says, "Train up a child in the way he should go; even when he is old he will not depart from it."

This verse encourages and reassures parents of the long-lasting impact of their efforts to guide and nurture their children in the right direction. It highlights the importance and value of the dedication and love you invest in your child's upbringing. By focusing on the principles of training and nurturing with love, you can find confidence and reassurance in your role as a mother, knowing that your efforts will have a lasting positive effect on your child's life.

- "My children are failures."

Jeremiah 29:11, "For I know the plans I have for you," declares the Lord, "plans to prosper you and not to harm you, plans to give you hope and a future."

This verse reminds us that God has a specific and prosperous plan for each individual, including our children. It emphasizes that God's intentions are to give hope and a bright future. Trusting in God's plans for your children can help you see their potential and purpose beyond any current struggles or setbacks, reinforcing the belief that they are not failures but are on a journey guided by God's good intentions.

- "My children don't appreciate me."

Galatians 6:9, "Let us not become weary in doing good, for at the proper time we will reap a harvest if we do not give up."

This verse encourages perseverance in doing good, even when it seems unappreciated or unnoticed. It reassures us that our efforts in nurturing and caring for our children will ultimately bear fruit. By continuing to show love and dedication, you can trust that your efforts are making a positive impact, even if the appreciation isn't immediately visible. This promise helps reinforce the value and importance of your role as a parent, encouraging you to keep going with faith and hope.

Lies About Your Career or Lack Thereof

- "I'm stuck in a dead-end job."

Colossians 3:23-24, "Whatever you do, work at it with all your heart, as working for the Lord, not for human masters, since you know that you will receive an inheritance from the Lord as a reward. It is the Lord Christ you are serving."

This verse encourages us to approach our work with dedication and heart, seeing it as a service to the Lord rather than merely a job. It reminds us that God values our efforts and that He has a greater reward and purpose for our work. By shifting our perspective to see our job as an opportunity to serve God, we can find meaning and fulfillment, regardless of the job's current status, and trust that God has a plan for our future.

- "I'll never be successful."

Joshua 1:8, "Keep this Book of the Law always on your lips; meditate on it day and night, so that you may be careful to do everything written in it. Then you will be prosperous and successful."

This verse emphasizes the importance of aligning our actions with God's word. It promises that we can achieve true prosperity and success by meditating on scripture and living according to its principles. It reassures us that success is not just about worldly achievements but also about living a life that honors God. By focusing on spiritual growth and obedience to God's guidance, we can trust that He will lead us to success in His perfect way and timing.

Lies About Money

- "I'll never be financially secure."

Philippians 4:19, "And my God will meet all your needs according to the riches of his glory in Christ Jesus."

This verse assures us that God is our ultimate provider and will supply all our needs. It emphasizes that God's provision is abundant and based on His glorious riches in Christ Jesus, not on our circumstances. By trusting in God's faithfulness and provision, we can overcome the fear of financial insecurity and have confidence that He will take care of us. This promise helps to shift our focus from our limitations to God's limitless resources and His ability to meet our needs.

- "I don't deserve wealth."

Deuteronomy 8:18, "But remember the Lord your God, for it is he who gives you the ability to produce wealth, and so confirms his covenant, which he swore to your ancestors, as it is today."

This verse reminds us that the ability to produce wealth comes from God and is part of His covenant with us. It emphasizes that wealth, when used according to God's principles, is a blessing and a tool for fulfilling His purposes. Recognizing that God is the source of our ability to generate wealth helps us see it as a gift from Him, dispelling the notion that we are undeserving. It encourages us to trust in God's provision and to use the resources He gives us responsibly and for His glory.

Lies About Health

- "I'll never be healthy."

Jeremiah 30:17, "But I will restore you to health and heal your wounds,' declares the Lord."

This verse offers a powerful promise of God's healing and restoration. It reassures us that no matter our current health challenges, God can restore and heal us. By trusting in His promise, we can find hope and encouragement, knowing that God can bring us back to health. This scripture helps us to shift our focus from our limitations and illnesses to God's ability to heal and renew us.

- "I'm too busy to take care of myself."

Mark 6:31, "Then, because so many people were coming and going that they did not even have a chance to eat, he said to them, 'Come with me by yourselves to a quiet place and get some rest.'"

This verse highlights the importance of rest and self-care despite busyness and demands. Jesus recognized the need for His disciples to take time away from their work to rest and rejuvenate. It reminds us that taking care of ourselves is essential for maintaining our well-being and effectiveness in our responsibilities. By following Jesus' example, we can prioritize self-care and find balance, ensuring that we are healthy and capable of fulfilling our roles effectively.

Lies About Your Home Environment

- "My home is always a mess."

Proverbs 24:3-4, "By wisdom a house is built, and through understanding it is established; through knowledge, its rooms are filled with rare and beautiful treasures."

This verse emphasizes that a well-ordered and beautiful home is built through wisdom, understanding, and knowledge. It encourages us to seek God's wisdom and guidance in managing our homes. Recognizing that a peaceful and orderly home is achieved through thoughtful and intentional actions can help shift our perspective. It reassures us that with God's help, we can create a nurturing and organized environment, even if it requires gradual and consistent effort.

- "I can't create a happy home."

Proverbs 3:33, "The Lord's curse is on the house of the wicked, but he blesses the home of the righteous."

This verse highlights that God blesses the home of the righteous, emphasizing that a happy and blessed home is rooted in living according to God's principles. We can invite His blessings into our home by seeking to live a life that honors God. It reassures us that creating a happy home is possible when we align our lives with God's will, seek His guidance, and foster an environment of love, respect, and faith.

Lies About Other Areas of Life

- "I'll never find balance in my life."

Matthew 11:28-30, "Come to me, all you who are weary and burdened, and I will give you rest. Take my yoke upon you and learn from me, for I am gentle and humble in heart, and you will find rest for your souls. For my yoke is easy, and my burden is light."

This passage invites us to come to Jesus with our burdens and promises rest and relief. It emphasizes that by learning from Him and taking on His yoke, we can find a sense of balance and peace in our lives. Jesus' yoke is described as easy and light, indicating that He provides a way of living that brings rest and alleviates the overwhelming pressures we may feel. Trusting in His guidance and following His example can help us achieve the balance we seek.

- "I'm always going to struggle."

Romans 8:37, "No, in all these things we are more than conquerors through him who loved us."

This verse reassures us that, through God's love, we are more than conquerors, overcoming life's challenges and struggles. It emphasizes that our struggles do not define us and that we can prevail over adversity with God's strength and love. Trusting in this promise helps us to shift our perspective from a mindset of perpetual struggle to one of victory and resilience through Christ.

CHAPTER 9 PROPHECY AND DECLARATIONS: SPEAKING LIFE OR DEATH INTO YOUR FUTURE

"Keep this Book of the Law always on your lips; meditate on it day and night, so that you may be careful to do everything written in it. Then you will be prosperous and successful."

— JOSHUA 1:8

Imagine stepping onto the stage of life, microphone in hand. Before you, a crowd of experiences, dreams, and moments yet to unfold. What if I told you that this microphone—your words— has the power to shape the soundtrack of your life? Too often, we underestimate the influence of our spoken words, dismissing them as mere whispers in the wind. Yet, Scripture and science alike highlight a profound truth: our tongues have the power to build worlds or burn bridges. In this chapter, let's explore how we can harness this divine instrument to orchestrate a life that resonates with God's promises and blessings.

9.1 THE POWER OF THE TONGUE: BIBLICAL FOUNDATIONS FOR SPEAKING LIFE

Scriptural Evidence of Speech Impact

Proverbs 18:21 compellingly states, "Death and life are in the power of the tongue," highlighting the profound influence our words possess. Similarly, James 3:5-10 likens the tongue to a tiny rudder that guides a large ship, emphasizing its potential to shape our life's direction. These passages are not mere figurative expressions; they offer divine wisdom on the actual effects that our words can have. Just as an avid gardener uses words to ward off certain pests and encourages plant growth, we possess the power to nurture our spiritual health and mental well-being through the words we speak.

Theological Interpretation

So, what does it really mean to speak life? It's about more than just avoiding gossip or negativity; it's about actively using our words to mirror God's truth in our lives and the lives of others. When we declare words of hope, peace, and joy, we are not just wishing for a better reality; we are aligning ourselves with God's creative power, who spoke the universe into existence. Our words have the capacity to initiate change, inspire action, and invoke divine intervention. By speaking life, we participate in the ongoing creation story, sowing seeds of blessing that can grow into tangible manifestations of God's goodness.

Historical Contexts

Looking back, biblical figures knew the weight of words.

Joshua: Declaring the Fall of Jericho

- Joshua 6:16, Joshua declares, "Shout! For the Lord has given you the city!"

When Joshua led the Israelites to the fortified city of Jericho, he received a divine strategy from God. His declaration was not a mere hope but a prophetic utterance rooted in God's promise. The Israelites followed God's instructions, and on the seventh day, the walls of Jericho fell, and they took the city. Joshua's words, spoken in faith, precipitated a miraculous victory.

David: Proclaiming Victory Over Goliath

- 1 Samuel 17:45-47, David said to Goliath, "You come against me with sword and spear and javelin, but I come against you in the name of the Lord Almighty, the God of the armies of Israel, whom you have defied. This day, the Lord will deliver you into my hands."

Despite Goliath's intimidating stature and the fear he instilled in the Israelite army, David boldly proclaimed victory. His declaration, founded on his unwavering faith in God's power, led to a stunning victory over the giant, demonstrating the effectiveness of speaking faith into seemingly impossible situations. These stories teach us that our words can and should be used to echo God's promises, to speak truth into the shadows of doubt, and to declare light into the darkness.

Practical Guidance

Now, how can you cultivate this habit of speaking life? Start by being mindful of the words that come out of your mouth. Become acutely aware of your daily speech patterns. What are you declaring over your life, your circumstances, and your future?

Begin each day with a declaration of truth—find a scripture that resonates with your current situation and speak it out loud. For instance, if you're facing uncertainty at work, declare Romans 8:37, "I am more than a conqueror through Christ who loves me." It's about setting the tone for your day, not based on what you see but on what God says.

Next, integrate this practice into your interactions. Choose to affirm, encourage, and uplift others with your words. Make your conversations a fountain of life, not a drain of vitality. When you face challenges, resist the urge to speak negativity. Instead, declare the outcome you hope for based on God's promises. Again, this isn't about denying reality but about defining reality through the lens of faith and God's unchanging truth.

By harnessing the power of your tongue, you wield the power to change your world. So, take hold of this divine instrument and let your words be the paint with which you color your life's canvas. Speak boldly, speak beautifully, speak life.

9.2 PROPHESYING YOUR FUTURE: HOW TO SPEAK GOD'S PROMISES INTO EXISTENCE

Have you ever considered yourself a prophet? No, I'm not suggesting you start wearing a robe and parting your local river, but what if I told you that you have the power to shape your future through the divine act of prophetic declaration? Prophecy doesn't always mean foretelling the future in a mystical sense; more often, it's about aligning our spoken words with God's eternal truth, bringing His promises to life in our present circumstances. It involves speaking God's truth into specific situations. It's less about predicting the future and more about declaring God's will, which can indeed shape the future.

For example, when Ezekiel spoke to the dry bones in Ezekiel 37, he wasn't just hoping for a miracle; he was actively participating in one by declaring God's life-giving words over what seemed hopelessly dead. This act of speaking life is a form of prophecy that we are all invited to engage in. It's about looking at your life, however dry or desperate it may seem, and speaking God's promises of life over it with authority and faith.

Steps to Prophetic Declarations

Creating and declaring prophetic words over your life is like planting seeds in a garden. You must choose the right seeds (God's word), plant them in faith, and nurture them by believing, praying and affirming them to see the fruits. Here's how you can start:

1. Identify the Need: Identify areas in your life that need transformation or divine intervention. Maybe you need healing, a financial breakthrough, or relationship restoration.
2. Find Scriptural Promises: Once you've pinpointed the areas of need, search the Scriptures for God's promises concerning these issues. These promises are your spiritual seeds.
3. Craft Your Declarations: Turn these scriptures into first-person declarations. For healing, you might declare, "By His stripes, I am healed." Make these declarations specific, positive, and in the present tense to affirm their current and active influence in your life.
4. Speak with Authority: When you declare these words, do so with conviction and faith, believing in God's power to

bring them to fruition. Speak them aloud daily, watering these seeds with the certainty of faith.

Role of Faith in Prophecy

Faith is the soil in which the seeds of your prophetic declarations grow. Without faith, these seeds lie dormant, but with faith, they flourish. Hebrews 11:1 defines faith as the assurance of things hoped for, the conviction of things not seen. In a prophetic declaration, your faith stands on the assurance that God's promises are true and reliable, even when the immediate evidence may suggest otherwise. It's believing that your declarations will not return void but will accomplish what they say because they are aligned with God's Word. The world teaches us to see it to believe it. Faith teaches us to believe it so we can see it.

Life Stories of Transformation

Consider the story of Anna, a woman who struggled with chronic illness for years. Doctors gave little hope, but instead of succumbing to despair, Anna began to declare daily, "I am strong and healthy because God heals all my diseases." Over time, not only did her health improve, but her faith grew exponentially. Similarly, Tina faced financial ruin after a business failure. She clung to Philippians 4:19, declaring, "My God supplies all my needs according to His riches in glory." Within a year, she experienced miraculous financial breakthroughs and was able to start a new, successful venture.

These stories exemplify the power of prophetic declaration. It's not about denying reality but about defining reality through the lens of God's truth. By speaking His promises into existence, you participate in unfolding His will in your life, turning the dry bones of your circumstances into an army of hope and fulfillment. So, grab hold of this divine privilege and start speaking God's transformative truths into your life today. Watch as the landscape of your future blossoms with the beauty of His promises fulfilled, one declaration at a time.

9.3 DAILY DECLARATIONS FOR HEALTH, PROSPERITY, AND JOY

Crafting effective declarations is like choosing vibrant, hopeful hues to create the day ahead. It's about intentionally selecting words that align with God's promises for health, prosperity, and joy and using them to color every corner of your life. Let's dive into how you can mix your palette of powerful declarations and incorporate them into the rhythm of your daily life, transforming your routine into a masterpiece of faith and positivity.

Crafting Effective Declarations

Creating powerful declarations begins with grounding them in the truth of God's Word. This isn't about wishful thinking or whimsical affirmations; it's about anchoring your hopes and dreams in the promises God has laid out in Scripture. Start by identifying areas where you desire growth or healing—physical health, financial stability, or emotional joy. Then, scour the Bible for verses that speak to these desires. For instance, if you're seeking health, Jeremiah 30:17 declares, "For I will restore health to you, and your wounds I will heal declares the Lord." Use this scripture to craft a personalized declaration like, "I am receiving God's healing; my health is being restored."

The key here is specificity and personal connection. Your declarations should resonate deeply with your personal struggles and aspirations, transforming general promises into personal proclamations that you can speak over your life with authority and faith.

Examples of Daily Declarations

To get you started, here are a few sample declarations that you can adapt and incorporate into your daily routines:

- For Health: "By His stripes, I am healed. Every cell in my body vibrates with energy and health (Isaiah 53:5)."
- For Prosperity: "God is supplying all my needs according to His riches in glory in Christ Jesus. I am financially free and abundant (Philippians 4:19)."
- For Joy: "The joy of the Lord is my strength. Today, I choose happiness over worry, and peace over despair (Nehemiah 8:10)."

Feel free to tweak these to suit your circumstances or scriptural preferences better. The more personalized your declarations, the more potent they become.

Integrating Declarations into Daily Life

Incorporating these declarations into your daily life can be as natural as your morning cup of coffee. One seamless method is to include them in your morning routine. As you brush your teeth or take your shower, recite your declarations. This sets a positive tone for your day and ensures that you start your morning empowered by God's Word.

Another practical moment for declarations is during your commute. Instead of tuning into the sometimes dreary news or mindlessly scrolling through social media, turn your travel time into a moment of spiritual affirmation. Speak your declarations out loud, declare them over your life, and visualize them taking root. Similarly, meal times can serve as excellent reminders to declare blessings over your food, your body, and your life—transforming routine meals into moments of gratitude and expectation.

Documenting Changes

Keep a journal of your journey to capture the impact of your daily declarations. Think of it as a documentary of your dialogue with destiny. Record the declarations you use, the dates you start, and any changes you notice in your health, mood, or circumstances. Over time, this journal will serve as a testament to God's faithfulness and a motivational reminder of the power of your words. Seeing the tangible effects of your declarations can strengthen your faith and encourage you to continue, even on days when the results aren't immediately apparent.

By weaving declarations into the fabric of your daily life, you are not merely hoping for change; you are speaking it into existence. Each word you declare is a thread in the tapestry of your future, colored with the hues of health, prosperity, and joy. So, grab your spiritual paintbrush and start transforming your life with the vibrant colors of God's promises. Speak boldly, believe confidently, and watch your world change one declaration at a time.

9.4 CELEBRATING VICTORIES: RECOGNIZING AND PROCLAIMING GOD'S GOODNESS

Let's pop the confetti and crank up the celebration playlist, shall we? In the hustle of everyday life, especially in moments when the to-do list seems like a never-ending scroll, taking time to celebrate victories—both big and small—can feel like a luxury we can scarcely afford. Yet, acknowledging and celebrating your victories isn't just about giving yourself a pat on the back. It's a fundamental practice that nourishes your spirit, bolsters your faith, and paints your life's canvas with vibrant, joyous colors. Whether it's overcoming a longstanding fear, reaching a personal goal, or witnessing a breakthrough in your spiritual journey, each victory is a testament to God's active presence and goodness in your life. So why not shout it from the rooftops?

Importance of Acknowledging Victories

Psychologically, celebrating achievements can significantly boost your morale, enhance your self-esteem, and propel you with renewed energy toward your next goal. Spiritually, it reinforces your trust in God's providence and timing, reminding you and those around you of His faithfulness and your growth. Each time you celebrate a victory, you're essentially weaving a narrative of gratitude and faith that strengthens your spiritual foundation and encourages others. It's a way of documenting God's fingerprints in your life, a spiritual journal that comes alive with each celebration.

Ways to Celebrate Achievements

Celebrations can be as unique as the victories themselves, and they don't always have to involve grand gestures (though those are fun too!). Sharing your testimony is a powerful way to celebrate. Whether within a community group, through social media, or over coffee with a friend, sharing the story of your victory can magnify the sense of achievement and simultaneously inspire others. Consider creating a 'Victory Wall' in your home—maybe a bulletin board or a digital slideshow—where you pin photos, notes, or items that symbolize your achievements. Each glance at this wall can be a heartwarming reminder of your journey and God's guidance.

For those who love to create, why not craft a victory song, poem, or piece of art? These creative expressions not only celebrate your victories but also serve as lasting reminders of those triumphant moments. And for those who appreciate a communal vibe, organizing a 'Praise Potluck' where friends and family come together to share food and stories of victory can turn individual achievements into a collective celebration of God's goodness.

Scriptures for Celebration

As you celebrate, anchor your joy in the Word of God, which offers numerous verses that resonate with the heart of celebration.

- Psalms 150:6, "Let everything that has breath praise the Lord. Praise the Lord!"

This verse invites all creation to join in a chorus of celebration, emphasizing that praise is a natural expression of life itself.

- Philippians 4:4, "Rejoice in the Lord always; again I will say, Rejoice."

This scripture calls us to maintain a spirit of joy rooted in our relationship with God, regardless of our circumstances.

So, as you move forward, remember to pause and celebrate. Let each victory, no matter how small, be a crescendo of joy in your life's symphony. Share your triumphs, document your progress, and let your life be a living testimony of God's endless goodness. After all, every victory is a brushstroke in the masterpiece God is painting with your life.

9.5 SETTING SPIRITUAL GOALS: DECLARATIONS FOR PERSONAL AND SPIRITUAL GROWTH

Intentional spiritual goals shape our faith journey and permeate every aspect of our lives with divine purpose and fulfillment.

Defining Spiritual Goals

So, what exactly are spiritual goals? Unlike career goals that might focus on climbing the corporate ladder, or fitness goals aimed at running a marathon, spiritual goals are about deepening your relationship with God and aligning your daily walk with His will. These could range from increasing your understanding of the Bible, enhancing your prayer life, or actively serving in your church or community. The beauty of spiritual goals lies in their ability to transform one aspect of your life and infuse other areas with greater meaning and connection to your faith.

Think of spiritual goals as the anchors that keep your soul grounded in stormy seas. They help you focus on what truly matters amid life's distractions and challenges. Whether it's committing to daily devotions, memorizing scripture, or leading a small group, each goal serves as a stepping stone towards a more profound spiritual maturity and a closer relationship with God.

Using Declarations to Support Goals

So how can we supercharge these goals? By using declarations. Declarations are not just wishful thinking; they are faith-filled statements that activate God's promises and power in our lives. For instance, if your goal is to become more patient and understanding, your declaration might be, "I am filled with love and patience through the Holy Spirit." By speaking this out loud daily, you affirm God's work in your life, transforming your mindset and actions to align with your spiritual aspirations.

Monitoring Progress

What's a goal without a way to track progress? Spiritual growth can sometimes feel intangible, but by setting markers, you can see just how far you've come. A spiritual journal can be a fantastic tool here. Regular entries about your experiences, challenges, and victories provide insight into your spiritual development and can be incredibly encouraging on days when progress feels slow. Alternatively, consider an accountability partner or a mentor who can provide objective feedback, encourage you, and celebrate your victories along the way.

Adjusting Goals and Declarations

As you grow in your faith, so will your goals and declarations. Not meeting all goals doesn't mean you've failed or fallen short; it simply means you are ready for new challenges and deeper growth. Periodically evaluate your goals—maybe every six months or at the end of each year. Ask yourself: Are these goals still stretching me? Are they drawing me closer to God? Adjust as necessary, and craft new declarations that reflect your current spiritual aspirations and the next level of your faith journey.

By setting specific, measurable, and timely spiritual goals supported by powerful declarations, you create a dynamic framework for spiritual growth that can propel you toward a deeper, more fulfilling relationship with God. These practices enable you to live out your faith actively and purposefully, making every day a step closer to the person God has called you to be.

SHARING THE KNOWLEDGE

Now that you have more understanding and practical tools to help you conquer toxic thoughts and embrace life with transforming truths, it's time to pass on your newfound knowledge and show other readers where they can find the same help.

Simply by leaving your honest opinion of this book on Amazon, you'll show other women where they can find the information they're looking for, and also enjoy peace and victory.

Thank you for your help. The mission of equipping girls and women with truth and practical tools to overcome toxic thoughts is kept alive when we pass on our knowledge – and you're helping me to do just that.

Scan this QR code to leave your review on Amazon.

CONCLUSION

"And they overcame him by the blood of the Lamb and by the word of their testimony...."

— *REVELATIONS 12:11*

So, here we are at the end of our shared journey—a journey that began with the first uncertain steps toward recognizing those pesky, unhelpful thoughts that so often clutter our minds. Together, we've navigated the tangled woods of toxic thinking and discovered powerful tools to recognize these intruders and send them packing with the truth of Scripture and the wisdom of science.

We've covered substantial ground. From understanding the anatomy of a toxic thought to embracing the neuroscience of belief, each chapter was a step toward freedom. We learned to counter common lies with the power of Scripture, use our understanding of the brain's plasticity to transform our thought patterns and lean on many stress-relief techniques that marry faith with scientific insight.

The vision of this book was, and remains, to empower you to conquer those toxic thoughts and step into a life marked by peace, joy, and fulfillment—a life that flourishes under the truths of Scripture, participates in God's Kingdom plan, and is supported by the best of what science can teach us about our minds and bodies.

We can find freedom from toxic thoughts by:

- Recognizing the lies that bind and blind.
- Taking every thought captive to make it obedient to Christ.
- Countering all lies with the truth of God's Word.
- Implementing practical, scientifically backed strategies to reinforce these truths.
- Transforming our minds, knowing that each small change contributes to a significant spiritual and mental renewal.
- Shifting the focus of our minds from our circumstances to God
- Embracing gratitude, grace, and forgiveness.
- Staying connected to the body of Christ where we can build community with like-minded fellow believers.

Now, I encourage you—no, I urge you—to put these strategies into practice. Make them a part of your daily routine. The road to transformation requires consistent effort, but remember, you are not laboring in vain. The work you are doing is building you up, renewing you day by day into the magnificent creation God designed you to be.

Share your journey. Let your testimony be the light that guides others who might still be struggling in the shadows of doubt and toxic thinking. There's a community of believers who can find hope and encouragement in your story—just as you might find inspiration in theirs.

Remember that you are a unique masterpiece, intricately designed and purposed by God. This journey through the pages of this book transcends mere self-improvement—it's a divine invitation to evolve into the entirety of your God-given potential. Remember, this path is not one you walk alone. Together, we stand, fortified by our shared faith, uplifted by our collective community, and steadfastly supported by the unyielding embrace of our Heavenly Father.

And now, let me leave you with this prayer:

> *Heavenly Father, thank You for our journey through these pages. Thank you for the spiritual insights and wisdom we have gleaned. I ask for Your strength and wisdom as we apply these truths daily to our lives. Help us to see ourselves as You see us—free, whole, and wonderfully made. Father I pray that you would guide us as we continue to combat the lies that seek to ensnare us, and fill our hearts and minds with Your peace as we live out Your truths. May we be lights in the darkness, spreading hope and love as we walk in the freedom You provide, and may we all walk in liberty and the power of your Holy Spirit as we advance your Kingdom here on earth as it is in heaven. In Jesus' name, Amen.*

Go forth in faith, beloved sister, armed with truth and love, and make your life a testament to the transformative power of God's Word and His unending grace.

BIBLIOGRAPHY

A Christian look at anxiety and depression: A testimony. (2019, June 11). Fight Off Faith. https://fightoffaithblog.com/2019/06/11/anxiety-depression-and-the-christian/

Bible Gateway. (n.d.). New International Version. https://www.biblegateway.com/

Beautiful examples of the fruit of the spirit - Answered Faith. (n.d.). Answered Faith. https://answeredfaith.com/beautiful-examples-fruit-spirit/

Carol Dweck on how growth mindsets can bear fruit in... (n.d.). Association for Psychological Science. https://www.psychologicalscience.org/observer/dweck-growth-mindsets

Harrison Taylor, K. Urban community garden practices as indicators of community social resilience. https://core.ac.uk/download/511345033.pdf

Helping people, changing lives: 3 health benefits of volunteering. (n.d.). Mayo Clinic Health System. https://www.mayoclinichealthsystem.org/hometown-health/speaking-of-health/3-health-benefits-of-volunteering#:

How gratitude changes you and your brain. (n.d.). Greater Good Science Center at UC Berkeley. https://greatergood.berkeley.edu/article/item/how_gratitude_changes_y ou_and_your_brain

How to choose a life verse. (n.d.). Crosswalk.com. https://www.crosswalk.com/faith/spiritual-life/how-to-choose-a-life-verse.html

Let God change your mind. (n.d.). In Touch Ministries. https://www.intouch.org/read/articles/let-god-change-your-mind

Neurotheology: The relationship between brain and religion. (n.d.). National Center for Biotechnology Information. https://www.ncbi.nlm.nih.gov/pmc/articles/PMC3968360/

Perfectionism and mental health problems: Limitations and... (n.d.). National Center for Biotechnology Information. https://www.ncbi.nlm.nih.gov/pmc/articles/PMC9125265/

Reduce stress and anxiety with Bible meditation - Abide. (n.d.). Abide. https://abide.com/blog/reduce-stress-and-anxiety-with-bible-meditation/

Religiously integrated cognitive behavioral therapy. (n.d.). National Center for Biotechnology Information. https://www.ncbi.nlm.nih.gov/pmc/articles/PMC4457450/

Self-affirmation activates brain systems associated with... (n.d.). National Center for Biotechnology Information. https://www.ncbi.nlm.nih.gov/pmc/articles/PMC4814782/

Setting healthy boundaries in the Bible - Therapy for Christians. (n.d.). Therapy for Christians. https://www.therapyforchristians.com/blog/boundaries-in-the-bible#:

The benefits of women's social ties for physical, psychological... (n.d.). PubMed. https://pubmed.ncbi.nlm.nih.gov/36440568/#:

The Bible and women? We need to talk | Reflections. (n.d.). Yale Divinity School. https://reflections.yale.edu/article/resistance-and-blessing-women-ministry-and-yds/bible-and-women-we-need-talk

The psychology of self-affirmation: Sustaining the integrity of the self. (n.d.). ScienceDirect. https://doi.org/10.1016/S0065-2601(08)60229-4

The sanctuary course. (n.d.). Sanctuary Mental Health Ministries. https://sanctuarymentalhealth.org/sanctuary-course/

Top 10 tips to learn how to mentor someone spiritually. (n.d.). Jayme Lee Hull. https://www.jaymeleehull.com/top-10-best-helpful-tips-for-the-christian-mentor-getting-started/

Understanding mental health: Definition, significance, and overcoming stigma | Self-care and mental well-being | Caring for nurses and caregivers. (n.d.). Health Overdose. https://healthoverdose.com/understanding-mental-health-definition-significance-and-overcoming-stigma/

Unpacking the relationship between prayer and anxiety. (n.d.). National Center for Biotechnology Information. https://www.ncbi.nlm.nih.gov/pmc/articles/PMC9713100/

Use this 5-step neurocycle to ease mental spirals. (n.d.). Well+Good. https://www.wellandgood.com/5-step-neurocycle

What does a sound theology of mental health look like? (n.d.). The Gospel Coalition. https://in.thegospelcoalition.org/article/theology-of-mental-health/#:

What is contemplative prayer and how... (n.d.). Guided Christian Meditation. https://guidedchristianmeditation.com/2515/meditation/what-is-contemplative-prayer-and-how-to-do-a-contemplative-prayer-practice/

Why your testimony matters. (2023, February). The Rebelution. https://www.therebelution.com/blog/2023/02/why-your-testimony-matters/

100 best Christian women blogs and websites in 2024. (n.d.). Feedspot. https://christian.feedspot.com/christian_women_blogs/

145 inspiring journal prompts for your mental well-being – The Fifth Element Life. (n.d.). The Fifth Element Life. https://thefifthelementlife.com/mental-well-being/

25 biblical affirmations to build your confidence &... (n.d.). Adorned in Armor. https://adornedinarmor.com/biblical-affirmations/

Any anxiety disorder. (n.d.). National Institute of Mental Health. https://www.
    nimh.nih.gov/health/statistics/any-anxiety-disorder

A powerful prayer to break generational curses. (n.d.). Crosswalk.com. https://
    www.crosswalk.com/faith/prayer/a-prayer-to-break-generational-curses.html

How do I heal from emotional abuse? (n.d.). Leslie Vernick. https://leslievernick.
    com/blog/how-do-i-heal-from-emotional-abuse/

60 Bible verses for anxiety - Choosing Therapy. (n.d.). Choosing Therapy. https://
    www.choosingtherapy.com/bible-verses-for-anxiety/